DATE DUE

8.96

AP 1 '88	JUL 1 1 '95		
JY 25 '88	FE 09 '06		
JE 27 '89	DE 14 '10		
OC 23 '89			
AG 8 '91			
NO 11 '91			
AG 7 '92			
AG 18 '92			
SE 14 '[illegible]			
AP 7 '93			
MY 4 '93			
MAR 15 '99			

Harelson, Randy
Five hundred of the
greatest, most . . .

500 OF THE GREATEST MOST INTERESTING MOST EXCELLENT & MOST FUN Hints For KIDS

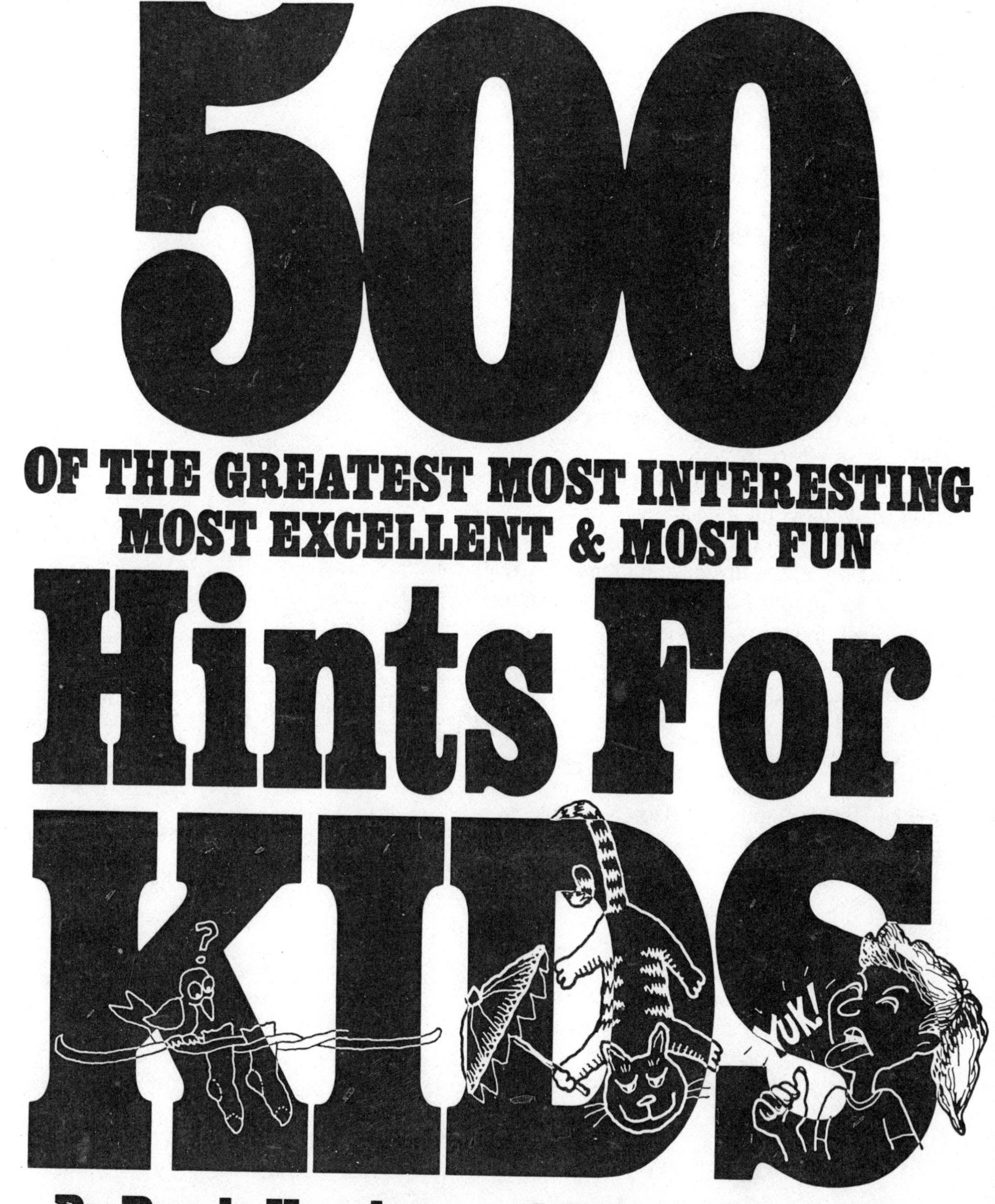

By Randy Harelson and Eileen Cavanagh

A Mary Ellen Family Book/Doubleday
Garden City, New York

500 OF THE GREATEST, MOST INTERESTING, MOST EXCELLENT AND MOST FUN HINTS FOR KIDS

Mary Ellen Family Books
6414 Cambridge Street
St. Louis Park, MN 55426-4461

ISBN 0-941298-15-9
Printed in the United States of America
First Printing:
10 9 8 7 6 5 4 3 2 1

Library of Congress Cataloging in Publication Data
Harelson, Randy.
500 of the greatest, most interesting, most excellent and most fun hints for kids.
"A Mary Ellen Family Book"
1. Amusements—Juvenile literature. 2. Creative activities and seat work—Juvenile literature. I. Cavanagh, Eileen. II. Title. III.: Five hundred of the greatest, most interesting, most excellent, and most fun hints for kids. IV. Title: Hints for kids. V. 500 Hints for Kids.
GV1203.H373 1984 790.1'922 83-14240
ISBN 0-385-19217-7

Art Directors: Randy Harelson & Cathleen Casey
Illustrations: Randy Harelson

Thanks for the hints.

To all the kids and adults who gave generously of their time, ideas, and encouragement, this book is affectionately dedicated.

The Allens
Richard Amadril
Gloria Andrade
Jill Artelet
Stacie Baxter
Annie Begrowicz
The Bergrens
Rena Bidney
Brian Blalock
Chris Blanch
Mark Bobrowski
Mrs. D. Bouford
Virginia and
  Jane Bowery
Diane Brady
Brown Elementary
  School kids
  Swansea,
  Massachusetts
Jackie Brown
Janet and Ray Bryan
Terry Bukaty
Gerri Cabral
Michelle Carden
Kitty Carew
The Carosellis
Amy Carter
Cathleen Casey
Brian Cavanagh
Peggy Cavanagh
Chris Champagne

Walter Charchalis
Renee Checchia
Joanna Cohen
Kim Courtemache
Catherine Davis
Carrie DesRosiers
Lisa DeWetter
Maureen Dezell
Jean Diemert
Danielle DiGiulo
Sandy and Paul Divine
Kristen Dochterman
Derek Donohue
Zelda Dorf
Lisa Dunbar
Jackie Duncan
Paula Fang MD
Faye Fleming
Carolyn Foley
Bill and Julie Fornaci
Richard Fuller
Lisa Furst
Richard Gibbs
Joseph Gilmartin III
Sandra Godwin
Debbie Goldman
Suzanne Gonzalez
Gwin Oaks School kids
  Lawrenceville,
  Georgia
Susan Hall

Darleen Hanby
Erika Hasenauer
Lynda Hatch
Carol Heepke
The Hodges
Sheri Holthus
Ellen and Joe Isacco
John Brown Francis
School kids,
Warwick,
Rhode Island
Carla Johnson
Burt Jordan DDS
Ruby Kalyanapu
Heather Keene
The Kings
Chris Kinnear
Mrs. Norman Krnavek
Steve Krug
Karen and
Richard Lambe
Steven Lamont
Stacy Langabeer
Jonathon and
Wendy Lazear
Sophia LeBlanc
Mary Maguire
The McCranns
Greg McDougall
Kate McLaughlin
Christina Mills
Melanie Milroy
Rick Morris
Penny Nask
Pam Nielson
North Kingstown
Free Library
librarians
Mary Norton
Tom Oberg
Peggy and
David O'Connor
Janice O'Donnell
Teri Oswald
Betty Owens
Dan and Tracy Pierce
Pilot Butte Junior High
School kids,
Bend, Oregon
Winsor Popoloski
John Prendergast
Mrs. S. Radoczy
Officer Jared Randall
Greg Rowland
Sally Russell
Jamie and Becky Sacco
John Sacco
St. Augustine
School kids,
Providence,
Rhode Island
St. Thomas School kids,
Phoenix, Arizona
Charlie Saunders
Rose and Bob Schindelar
Doug Schobel
Mrs. Melvin Schoen
Carol Seifert
Charlie Shaw
Bob Simister

Maria Sizer
Dave Souza
Kerri Steere
Stony Lane School kids
North Kingstown,
Rhode Island
Syna Stevenson
Chris Sturgeon
Claire Sweet
Ron Swenson
Chris Tomasino
Michael Thornton
Anne Timmons
The Trainors
Joe VanBenten
Greg Weiss MD
Wickford Elementary
School kids
North Kingstown,
Rhode Island
Willett Elementary
School kids
Attleboro,
Massachusetts
Karen Wilson
Annie Wittels

Special thanks to all the Cavanaghs, especially Helen and John, Paul and Max, Michelle, Bridget, Elizabeth, John, Emily and Billy, Mike and Liz, Jack and Carolyn, Kevin, Alan, and Nathan, and Tom (whose hints were not included). And to the Harelsons: Jack, Wessie, and Clint.

Table of Contents

When I was a kid I had trouble with keeping my shoelaces tied till I found out how to tie a double knot. Ever since I found out that first helpful hint I've been on the lookout for fast, easy, fun ways of solving everyday problems. And I've been sharing my hints with busy moms and dads in *Mary Ellen's Best of Helpful Hints* books.

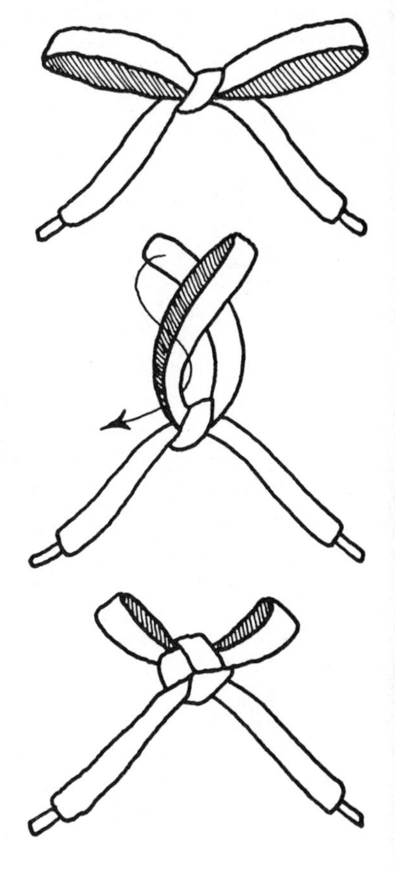

Now Randy Harelson and Eileen Cavanagh have put together *500 Hints for Kids* to make *your* busy life a little easier and a lot more fun. The authors collected hints from across America: from grandmothers, uncles, teachers, coaches, scout leaders, parents, and, best of all, kids themselves. Some of these hints are just for fun (travel pastimes or instant beanbags) and some are very important (what to do in an emergency or a lightning storm) and some will help you to do things better (drawing or baseball) but all of them are simple, practical, and fun to read.

So, open up *500 Hints for Kids*. It's chock-full of things to make, games to play, recipes, holiday celebrations, and hundreds of ideas for things to do and hints for how to do them.

Have fun!

Mary Ellen

P.S. Please be careful and use common sense when trying out new ideas.

Age

How Old Will You Be in 2000 A.D.?

Subtract the year you were born from 2000. The remainder will be your age in the year 2000.

Your Age in Days

How many days old will you be on your next birthday? Multiply 365.25 times the age you will turn. (The .25 accounts for Leap Day, February 29, which occurs every fourth year.)

Airplane Travel

For the Best View

At the airline check-in counter, ask for a window seat.

Bring Along Gum

Sometimes when flying in an airplane sudden changes in air pressure will cause the tubes in your middle ear to squeeze shut and for a few moments you won't be able to hear very well. You can usually open up the tubes again by yawning or swallowing or chewing gum.

Alarm Clocks

Trouble Getting Up on Time?

Put your alarm clock on the other side of the room so you *have* to get up to shut it off. Once you're up, go straight to the shower or have your breakfast or do jumping jacks, anything! But don't go back to bed.

Alarm Clocks

Late for Dinner?

You won't be late coming home from playing at a friend's house if you ask your friend to set an alarm clock to go off at the time you have to leave for home. (You can set a clock for your friend at your house too.) Put the clock in an open window if you're playing outdoors.

Animal Watching

Wildlife Walk

When you go on a walk to look for wildlife, keep the sun behind you so you can see animals clearly without sun in your eyes.

Wear soft-soled shoes and clothes that blend in with the colors of the environment.

Move quietly and steadily without talking, and "freeze" when you spot an animal.

Perhaps the best way to see wildlife is to find a comfortable spot and sit perfectly still for at least fifteen minutes. The animals will slowly venture out to look at *you*!

Waterscope

To see underwater creatures in a pond or stream, submerge a large glass jar halfway in the water and look down through the bottom. (Careful: it's breakable.)

Finding Addresses

To find the mailing address of any famous person go to your public library and ask the reference librarian for help.

Reply Requested

When writing to a famous person, if you want an autograph, say so. You'll be more likely to get it if you include with your letter a stamped enveloped addressed to yourself. The famous person can use the SASE (Self-Addressed Stamped Envelope) to send an autograph back to you.

Be Prepared

Serious autograph collectors always carry a pen and their autograph books when they go a concert, sports event, or anywhere they're likely to see a famous person.

Babysitting

The First Time's Free

If a new family moves into your neighborhood, offer to watch their kids for free while they unpack. If you do a good job, you may become their regular babysitter.

Babysitter's Bag of Tricks

Bring along a bag or a box of playthings the next time you go babysitting and use them to entertain the kids, especially when their parents are getting ready to leave. Here are some ideas for things to collect:

- ☐ Balls
- ☐ Crayons & paper
- ☐ Magazines
- ☐ Small boxes
- ☐ Costume jewelry
- ☐ Hand puppets
- ☐ Storybooks from the library

Babies Love Red

Wear bright colored clothes when you babysit. Babies love bright colors, especially red.

Mother's Helper

If you're not old enough to babysit by yourself, you can still be a babysitter by watching little kids when their parents are close by. A mother might want you to play with her baby while she's preparing dinner, playing tennis, or sewing, for example. Try volunteering your services.

Backpacks

Travel Light

To prevent fatigue and muscle strain you should keep your loaded backpack as light as possible—for most kids ten pounds is about right.

To weigh your backpack, first weigh yourself on a scale. Then put on your loaded pack and stand on the scale again. The difference between the first number and the second is the number of pounds your backpack weighs.

THE BACKPACK WEIGHS 8 POUNDS.

Keep It Comfortable

Pipe insulation (available at hardware stores) placed over the aluminum frame of your backpack makes it more comfortable to carry.

Also, carry clothes and soft stuff closest to your back.

Conserve energy while hiking by carrying your pack high on your shoulders and close to your body.

Balloons

Balloon Stretch

If a balloon is hard to blow up, stretch it a few times with your fingers and try again.

Another way to stretch it is to attach the opening of the balloon to a faucet and run some water into it (as if to make a water balloon). Let the water out and the balloon should be easier to blow up.

Balloons

Not With a Knot

A balloon can be used more than once if, instead of tying a knot, you slip a penny into the neck of the blown-up balloon to hold in the air. (Two people can do this more easily than one.)

Stuck by Static Electricity

Stick balloons to your wall or ceiling (especially for a party) by first rubbing them against your hair or wool sweater.

Band-Aids

No Ouch

Before pulling off a Band-Aid, rub it all over with some baby oil.

Baseball

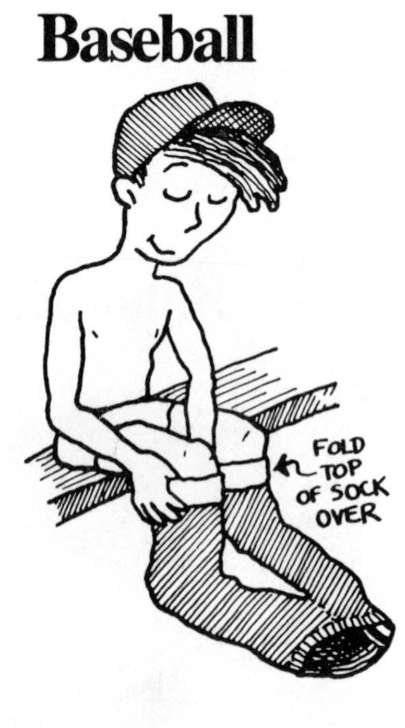

Pants Tip from the Pros

1. Before you put on your baseball pants, turn them inside out.
2. Put on your socks.
3. Pull the bottom of your pants up over socks, then fold about three inches of the top of the sock over the bottom of the pants.
4. Pull the pants up by the waist. (They'll turn right-side-out as you pull.)

Now they'll stay tight fitting at the knee and neat looking through a whole game.

Baseball

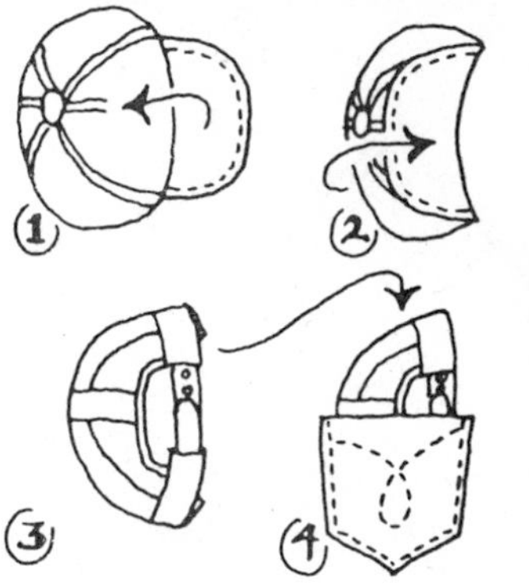

A Cap in Your Pocket

To carry your baseball cap in your back pocket without bending the visor, fold the visor up against the cap, then turn the cap inside-out making a little package with the visor inside.

Red Sox (or Any Color)

A rolled-up pair of socks makes a good indoor ball for pitch and catch or practicing aim. Set up a stuffed toy on a chair and try to knock it over.

Substitute Pitcher

Make a baseball tee for practice or a game.

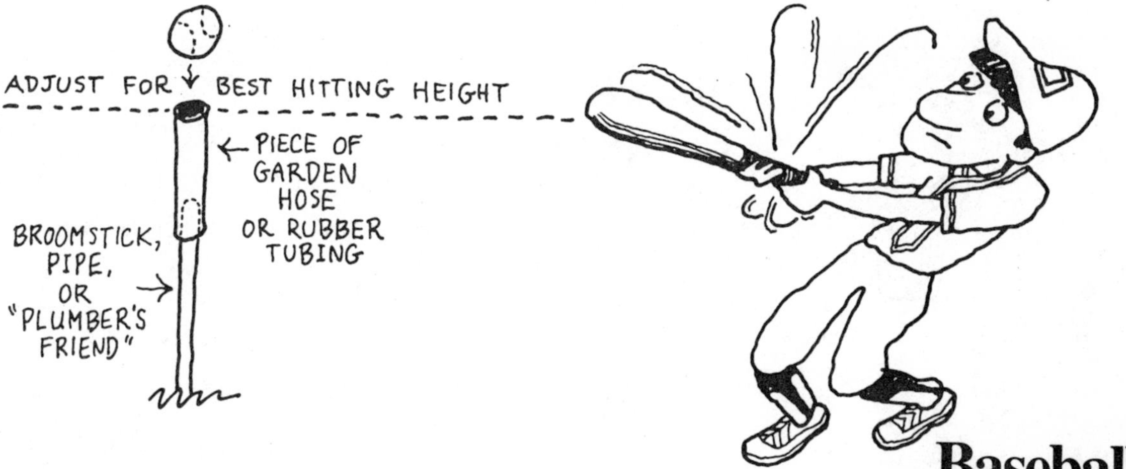

Baseball Cards

A Card in Your Cap

Put a baseball card inside the front of your baseball cap to help keep it from getting flat.

All-Stars

Just for fun, put together an all-star team from your collection of baseball cards.

Basketball

A Peach of a Basket

The first basketball hoop (in 1891) was a peach basket, and that's still a pretty good idea!

X Marks the Spot

If you don't have a hoop, make an X with masking tape on a high outdoor wall away from windows. Practice shooting your basketball to hit the spot.

High Speed/Low Control

Use a low bounce dribble for control and a high bounce dribble for speed.

Obstacle Court

To improve your ball control, set up obstacles (chairs, barrels, anything) on your driveway or playground and pretend they are players you must dribble around.

Sink It!

When you're shooting a foul shot in basketball, try this to improve your concentration:

1. Bounce the ball a few times.
2. Take a deep breath.
3. Exhale every bit of it.
4. Shoot.

Baths

Bubble Bath
For a tub full of bubbles, start running water for your bath, then pour in about a tablespoon of Lux or Ivory Liquid.

Skinned Knees
Newly skinned knees and elbows won't sting as much in the bath if you first coat the area lightly with petroleum jelly.

Tub Race
To get dressed and out of the bathroom quickly after taking a bath, unplug the drain and try to be out of the bathroom before the water drains out of the tub.

If You Need to Save Water . . .
A shower usually takes less water than a bath.

Beach

Sand Paper
Pick up almost any stick and use it to draw big pictures in the sand. Life-sized people, sea monsters and mermaids seem right at home on the beach and you rarely get a chance to draw pictures this large anywhere else.

Barefoot Blues
Get beach tar off your feet with a little suntan oil or mineral oil.

Beach

Treasure Hunt

Bring a magnet to the beach to see what metal treasures you might find in the sand.

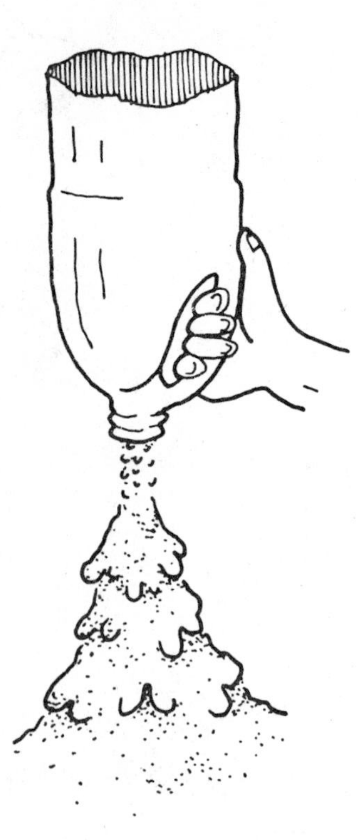

Beach Bottle

Cut off the bottom of an empty plastic bleach bottle to make a great beach toy. With the bottle cap on, it's a sand and water scoop. Or, take off the cap to use the bottle as a funnel to make dribble sand castles.

Dribble Castles

Dig a hole in the sand close to the ocean so that it fills up with water. Pick up wet sand from the hole and "dribble" it onto a pile to create fanciful towers and Christmas trees.

Instant Beach Chair

Push together piles of sand under your knees and behind your back to create a comfortable seat on the beach. "Upholster" your sand chair by laying a beach towel on top.

Beach

Mark Your Place

When you leave your belongings or friends to go for a walk down the beach, tie a colorful T-shirt or bandanna to a tall stick or pole and stick it in the sand. You can keep track of how far you have walked by looking back at your "flag".

Lost in the Sand

If you misplace something small on the beach, *do not* start digging—you might bury the lost object. Instead, stand up, walk around and look over the whole area carefully. Then, if you must check under the sand, sweep the surface gently with your hand.

Never bury anything valuable in the sand to hide it; you might hide it from yourself.

Beanbags

Full of Beans

When you need a beanbag but don't have one handy, just fill an old sock with dried beans and tie it in a knot.

Bees and Bugs

If Bees Bug You

Bees love blue. If bees bother you don't wear blue.

Bees love perfume. Leave if off when spending time outdoors.

If a bee lands on you, leave it alone. It will fly away on its own. It has no interest in harming you.

Bees and Bugs

If a Honeybee Stings

Scrape the stinger off immediately, being careful not to break or crush it. Dab the sting with wet baking soda or a half-and-half solution of household ammonia and water.

Or break open a cigarette. Wet the tobacco with water and press the sting with the tobacco. Caution: Some people are extremely allergic to the stings. Breaking out in hives, having trouble breathing, and swelling up in various parts of the body are danger signs that mean get to a doctor immediately.

If a Wasp Stings

Dab the sting with vinegar.

Out!

To get a bee or other insect out of your house or classroom:

1. Trap the insect against a wall or window by putting a juice glass over it.

2. Slide an index card or piece of stiff paper between the rim of the glass and the wall.
3. Hold the paper cover and carry the glass outdoors.
4. Release the insect.

Rust Removers

Rub chrome parts of your bike with aluminum foil to remove rust.

For even better results, put some cola on the aluminum foil first.

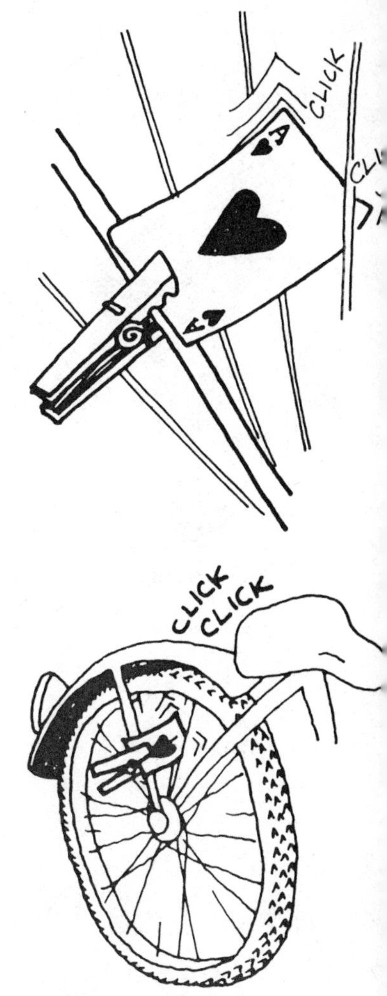

Shiniest Bike on the Block

To polish the chrome on your bike, mix equal parts baking soda and peanut butter and rub it thinly all over the chrome. After a minute or two polish it with a soft cloth. (Be careful to keep the polish out of the bike's moving parts.)

Motor Bike

To make your bike sound like it has a motor, clothespin a baseball card or playing card to one of the fender struts (the strut is a metal piece that holds the fender in place). The playing card should stick into the spokes just enough to make a clicking noise as the wheel turns.

Bicycle Gears Can be Catching

Put a rubber band around your pants leg to keep it from catching in the bike's gears.

Or tuck the cuff into your sock.

Or simply roll up your pants to your calf.

Bicycles

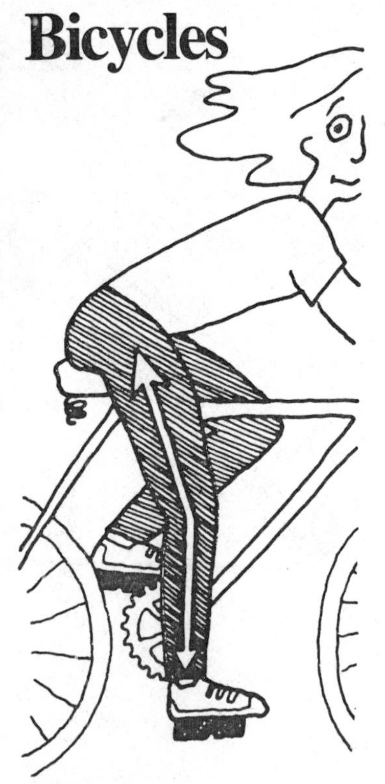

Conserve Energy

You'll save energy peddling your bike if you follow this tip: adjust the seat high enough that your leg is almost fully extended when the pedal is closest to the ground.

Cycle Safety

You may not have a driver's license, but when you ride your bike on public roads you should follow the same traffic laws as automobile drivers. Always ride on the right hand side of the road and remember that traffic lights, stop signs, one way streets, and so forth are for cyclists as well as drivers.

Bird Watching

Early Birds

The best time to see birds is early morning, 7 A.M. or before.

Easy Bird Call

Call birds to come see *you* by making a long kissy noise three times or saying "Pssh, pssh, pssh." Often, little birds will fly closer. . . maybe to see who's making that silly noise!

Bird Watching

Birdwatching from Bed

If you're sick for a few days, see if you can get someone to put your bed near a window with a bird feeder outside. Birds are fun to watch, and you'll learn a lot about the ones that live in your neighborhood.

Birthdays

First Thing!

For Mom or Dad's birthday, make a happy birthday poster and hang it on the refrigerator with tape or magnets first thing in the morning. Don't mention it—let it be a surprise.

Push-Button Birthday Song

If you have push-button telephone you can call up a friend on his or her birthday, say hi, and then play the song "Happy Birthday" by pushing the phone buttons in the folowing order:

Birthdays

Birthday Balloon in the Mail
Write a birthday greeting on a small sheet of paper, roll it up and slip it into a balloon. Mail the balloon in an envelope with instructions to "Blow up and pop!".

Half-Birthdays
If your birthday comes late in December you may feel overshadowed by all the other celebrating going on. If so, consider having your birthday party on your half-birthday in June.

Biting Your Nails

Break the Habit!
Set aside a special time every week to have someone give you a manicure. (Because if your nails look nice you'll think twice about biting them.)

In the morning, dig your fingernails lightly into a bar of soap. Nobody will see the soap, but your nails will taste terrible if you try to bite them.

Blow-Up Toys

To Find a Leak
To find a hole in an inflatable tire, air mattress, or beach ball, hold it underwater—bubbles will come up from the leak.

Draw a circle around the leak with chalk or crayon (both will draw underwater).

To Fix a Leak

Deflate the inflatable (in other words, let the air out). Clean and dry the area around the leak.

Two or three coats of nailpolish will usually repair tiny holes.

For bigger leaks buy repair tape or a repair kit at a store that sells inflatables.

Want to Read a Good Book?

Ask friends to tell you about their favorite books.

If you like a story by a certain author, you will probably like other stories he or she has written. Libraries shelve fiction books in alphabetical order by the author's last name so you'll usually find your favorite author's books together on the same shelf.

Tell the librarian what kind of book you'd like and the titles of other books you've enjoyed, and ask him or her for suggestions.

Books

A Kid's Best Charge Card

If you don't have one yet, head straight to your public library and ask for your own library card. With it you can borrow books, magazines, and, from some libraries, records, films, pictures, and even toys *free*. Your own "charge card" at no charge!

A Chapter a Night

If you get in the habit of reading at least one whole chapter of a book every night, you'll read a lot of books.

Bowling

Bowling Bottles

Empty plastic liter bottles (the kind soft drinks come in) make good bowling pins for at-home play. Use a Nerf ball or an inflated ball to "bowl them over".

Bowling Alley Etiquette

When bowlers in lanes next to each other approach at the same time, the person to the right should be allowed to bowl first.

Braces

Never Chew Gum with Braces, But . . .
If one of the wires of your braces ever comes loose or breaks and a sharp point starts poking into your cheek or gum, wad up some chewing gum and mold it over the sharp point. Then get to the orthodontist quickly.

Bubble Gum

Blow Bigger Bubbles
The secret of blowing big bubbles is to chew at least two pieces of bubble gum, together, for a long time. The longer you chew them, the softer and stretchier they become. The result: bigger bubbles!

A Sticky Mess
Get bubble gum off your face by dabbing it with the rest of the wad of gum.

Get gum out of your hair by rubbing it for a few minutes with peanut butter. The peanut butter loosens the gum and allows it to be pulled off gently.

Get gum off your clothes and shoes by rubbing it with an ice cube. When the gum is frozen it can be pulled or scraped off.

Cake Decorating

Words from Above

Writing on a cake with icing takes a bit of skill. An easier way to add words is to write on a paper "flag" with crayon or felt-tip pen. Attach the flag to a wooden skewer or plastic drinking straw; then stick it in the cake.

For Cakes that Rate

Decorate frosted cakes or cupcakes with animal crackers and small colorful candies.

Small wooden or plastic toys, washed and well-dried, also make great cake decoration.

To make little paper people, animals, and other figures for cake decorations, fold your paper first so you cut out a front and back at the same time. Glue toothpicks in between the front and back, leaving enough toothpick for sticking the decoration into the cake.

Push birthday candles into the centers of gumdrops or Life Savers, then arrange the candy candleholders on top of the cake.

Coconut Cover-up

If you ever make a mess of frosting a cake (such as the common problem of getting crumbs into the frosting), shake up shredded coconut with a little food coloring. Sprinkle it all over the cake for a fancy finish.

No Midnight Snacks

Keep raccoons and other critters from getting into your food, especially while you're sleeping. Put food in a nylon bag and hang it well off the ground from a tree branch.

Never keep food in your tent.

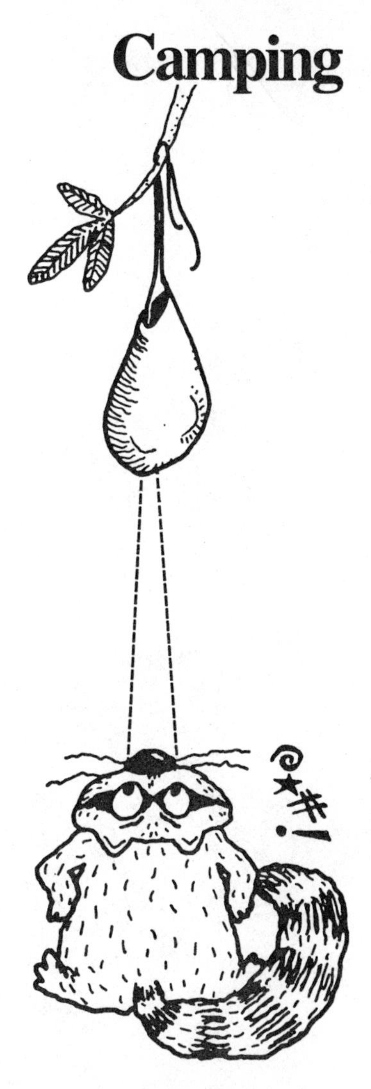

Ice Water

A day or so before you leave on a camping trip, fill some clean plastic jugs nearly full with water. Put them in the freezer. Just before you leave take them out and bring them along. That night and even the next morning you'll still have cold drinking water as the ice slowly melts.

This Clothes Line Needs No Pins

Wrap the middle of a long rope around a tree. Holding the two ends together, twist the rope several times around itself, then tie the ends around another tree. Hang damp clothes by slipping parts of them between the doubled rope.

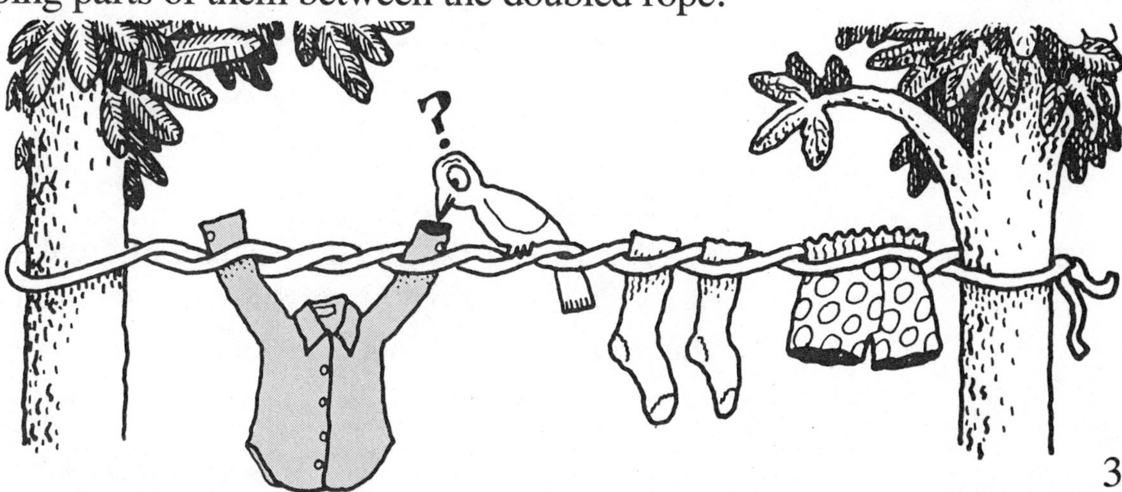

Camping

Ground Cover

A plastic tablecloth makes a good ground-cloth for keeping the earth's dampness out of your sleeping bag. If the tablecloth has flannel backing, place the flannel side up and you'll stay even warmer.

Cats

Here Kitty

Many cats will come running when they hear you shake the cat food box at the back door (or run the can opener if your cat eats canned food).

To Get Your Cat Down from a Tree. . .

Wait. She will always come down on her own. (Have you ever seen a cat's skeleton in a tree?)

Ping Pong for Puss

Put a ping pong ball or two in the bathtub (no water, please) and let your cat play in there.

Feline Football

Roll up a pair of worn out socks as a ball for your cat.

Cat at Bat

Attach a rubber ball, bell, or small unbreakable toy to a sturdy string. Hang this from a doorknob where your cat can bat it around.

Cat Salad

To prevent your cat from eating houseplants, plant some grass seed in a pot and place it with the other plants. Cats like grass and it's good for them.

No grass seed? Plant bird seed—most of it is grass.

Keep the Rind in Mind

Most cats love to eat cantaloupe rind. . . the part people throw away.

Just a Little Nip Tip

A grown cat will become like a kitten again when she gets a smell or a taste of catnip, a plant in the mint family. You can buy dried catnip or you can grow it from seed (available at any nursery). Plant it in your garden where you won't mind your cat rolling around in it (cats get pretty silly around this stuff!).

Chopsticks

Pick-Up Sticks

Most Chinese restaurants will give you chopsticks to eat with if you ask for them. Learn to use chopsticks by practicing with two pencils. Hold them like this:

Using the pencil chopsticks like tongs, pick up various small objects until you can do it without dropping them.

Christmas Trees

Keep Your Green Tree Green

A live-cut tree will stay fresher looking and keep its needles longer if you follow a few simple tips:

Keep the tree in a cool, dark place until it's time to decorate it.
Cut at least an inch off the bottom of the trunk before putting it into the Christmas tree stand.

Put a tablespoon of sugar in the tree's water supply, then check the water every few days. (While you're under the tree checking the water you can also check out which presents have your name on them!)

Popcorn Garlands

If you're planning to string old-fashioned popcorn garlands, pop the corn a few days ahead of time and leave it out to get stale. (Fresh popcorn will break when you push the needle through.)

For extra-pretty garlands alternate fresh whole cranberries and popcorn.

After Christmas hang popcorn and cranberry garlands on an outdoor shrub where birds can eat from them. (Birds don't mind stale popcorn.)

Just Add a Hanger

Fancy Christmas cookies and gingerbread people make tasteful (and tasty) tree ornaments if you remember to make holes at the top of each one *before* baking. (Pull colorful threads through the holes for hanging.)

Don't throw away those old toys you've outgrown. Small toys and dolls become wonderful tree ornaments with the simple addition of colorful ribbon or embroidery thread for hanging. After Christmas you can store them with the other ornaments to use again next year.

Inexpensive wooden or plastic fishing "bobs" or floats (available at any store with fishing supplies) become colorful Christmas balls when hung on the tree.

Attach delicate ornaments to the tree with twist ties (the kind that come with plastic garbage bags) especially at the bottom where a pet or a baby could knock them off.

By the way, an especially beautiful tree ornament (homemade or store-bought) is a nice gift. Wrap it up with a tag that says "Open *Before* December 25".

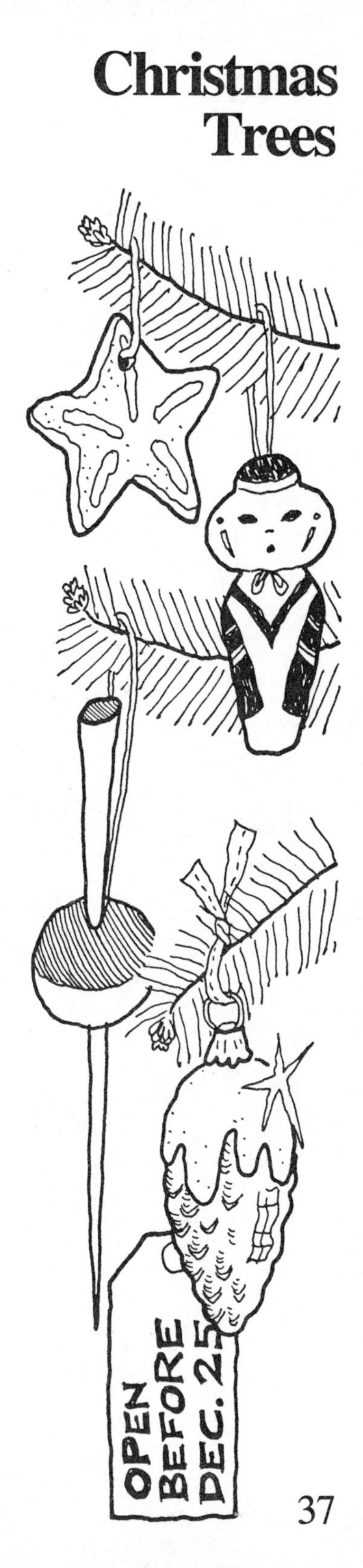

Clay

Soft Touch

Plastic modeling clay will stay soft and stretchy if you keep it in a covered container when you're not using it. An empty margarine tub with a plastic snap-on lid makes a good "clay closet". If you forget to put modeling clay away and it gets hard, put it in an empty container in the sun or near a light bulb. Heat softens modeling clay. (Sometimes, just kneading the clay in your hands will do the trick.)

Baker's Clay

Here's one recipe craftspeople use to make "bread dough" Christmas ornaments:

2 cups flour
1/2 cup salt
3/4 cup water

Mix all the ingredients in a bowl, then knead the dough for five minutes with well-floured hands. Create ornaments or small sculptures on a cookie sheet and bake in a 350° F oven for one hour or until completely dry.

This dough can be used as modeling clay for a long time if stored in a tightly closed plastic bag.

Cleaning Your Room

Six Ways to Make Cleaning Your Room More Fun

- ☐ Play your favorite record album or cassette tape and clean to the beat. Try to finish before the last song ends.
- ☐ Set the kitchen timer at how many minutes you think it will take to clean up, then try to finish before the timer rings.
- ☐ Pretend your wastepaper basket is a basketball hoop and shoot baskets to get rid of your trash.
- ☐ Have a friend help you clean your room, then help your friend clean his or her room.
- ☐ Ask your mom (or someone) to hide some buttons in your room and try to find them while you're cleaning up.
- ☐ Make believe there's a wicked witch who will lock you in the dungeon if you don't get every wrinkle out of your bed and every crumb off the floor.

Clothes

Button Up

Button shirts and coats from the bottom up; this way you can see the first button and buttonhole and be sure to come out even at the top.

No-Sew Hem

Here's a way to hem new pants without sewing: tape the hems to the inside of the pants with silver duct tape or masking tape.

Pulled-Out Drawstring

If you lose the end of a drawstring in a jacket or sweatshirt, pull out the string and attach a safety pin to one end. Use the safety pin to lead the drawstring back into place, working it through the hem from the outside with your fingers. Tie a knot at each end so the string can't be pulled out again.

Stop Running

Use a dab of nail polish to stop a run in your tights. Or rub the run with a bar of wet soap.

Coin Machines

Coin Returned?

If your coin keeps sliding out of a vending machine, rub it on your clothes a few times and try again. If that doesn't work, try another coin.

Cold Weather

Heat Rises
Since a lot of body heat is lost through the top of your head, you'll stay warmer if you wear a cap or hood outdoors.

Insulate!
Several layers of thin clothing will keep you warmer than just one heavy garment because layered clothing (for example an undershirt, shirt and sweater) traps air between the layers and acts as insulation.

Invisible Ski Mask
Rub a thin layer of petroleum jelly on your face before playing outdoors in very cold weather.

Collecting

Show and Tell
If you collect something special (such as stamps, baseball cards, matchbooks, postcards, stickers, dolls, or models) be sure to let your friends and relatives know what you collect. If they know what to look for, they may find items to add to your collection.

Color Mixing

Mix Master

When mixing two colors, it's a good idea to start with the lighter color and add the darker color a little at a time.

Yellow + Red = Orange
Yellow + Blue = Green
Red + Blue = Purple
White + Black = Gray
Red + Black = Brown
White + Red = Pink
White + Purple = Lavender

Never mix paints in the jars they come in. An empty egg carton holds twelve different colors, and you can just throw it away when you're through. Baby food jars are great for mixing and then storing paint colors you make.

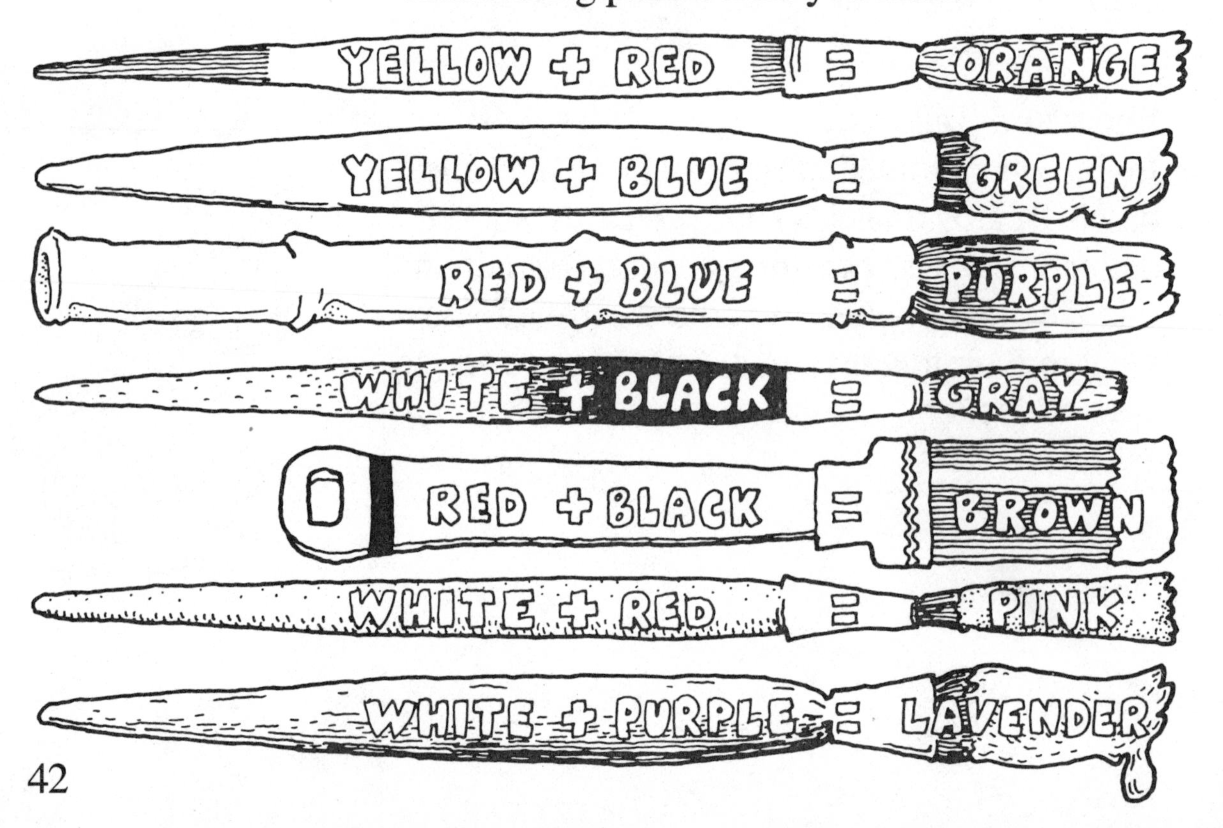

Color Mixing

Five Jars of Paint

If you buy tempera or any paint that comes in separate containers, you can get almost every color possible by buying only five colors of paint: red, blue, yellow, black, and white. Red, blue, and yellow are the primary colors and can be mixed to create every color in the rainbow. Black darkens colors. White lightens them up.

People Colored Crayon

To create light color flesh for your drawing of a person, color lightly with an orange crayon then color over it with white.

For darker flesh, color lightly with brown then color over it with white.

The white crayon mixes with the darker color to create a fairly realistic skin shade.

Shadows

Shadows are not black! A shadow is a darker shade of whatever color it is falling on. For example, the shadow of a tree on green grass is dark green. (Look at real shadows and you'll get the idea.)

Comic Book Box

Some cereal boxes and detergent boxes are just the right size for storing comic books.

Comics

Presto Change-O

Transfer a comic or other small newspaper picture onto a sheet of paper like magic! Make a mixture of one teaspoon dishwashing liquid and one teaspoon white vinegar. Use your finger to dab the mixture all over the picture. Put a piece of white paper over it and rub firmly with the back of a spoon. Pick up the white paper to see the transfer.

Cookie Cutters

Cut it Out

Cookie cutters will cut sliced bread as well as cookie dough. Use them for making fancy shaped sandwiches, French toast, and cinnamon toast.

Getting a Round

No metal cookie cutter is needed to make round cookies. Cut the dough with the rim of a juice glass first dipped in cold water or flour.

Crayons

All Wrapped Up

The paper wrapper around a crayon helps to keep it from breaking. Masking tape wrapped around the paper will protect the crayon even more.

Crayon "Wash"

For softer color, especially on large areas, take off the wrapper and color with the side of the crayon. For example, this is a good way to color a soft blue sky.

Crayons

Oil and Water Don't Mix

Color an area with crayon, rubbing hard but letting some paper show through here and there. Now go over the area with water-base paint or marker of a different color. The water-base color will stick to the paper but not to the crayon (because the crayon is oil-base) creating a sparkling color effect. (Just to experiment, color with a yellow crayon then go over it with red paint or marker.)

Crayons or Colored Pencils?

Crayons are great for quickly coloring large, bright shapes and areas in simple drawings. Fine point pens and colored pencils are better for small, detailed drawings that take more time. Feel free to use several art materials in the same drawing.

Cutting With Scissors

Are You Left-Handed?

Left-handed people usually find it easier to cut *clockwise* around a shape.

Right-handed people usually find it easier to cut *counterclockwise* around a shape.

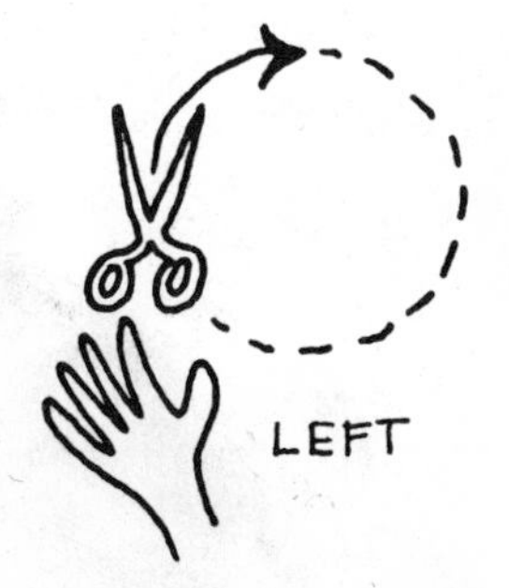

Cutting With Scissors

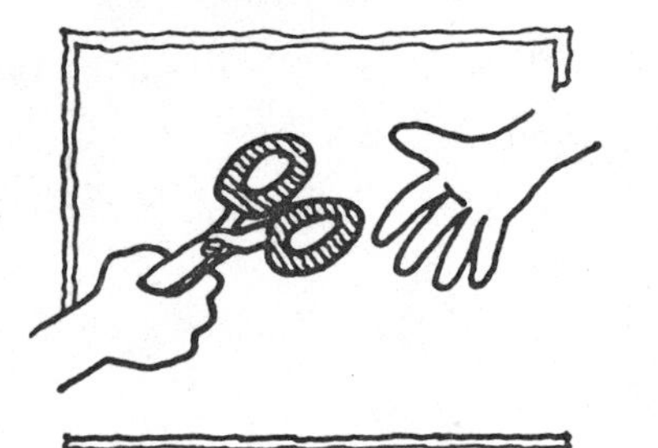

Real Sharp!

Sharpen school scissors by cutting lines into a piece of fine sandpaper.

For Safety's Sake

Always hand scissors to someone else handles first.

Keep it Simple

When cutting out a complicated shape, cut a simple shape all the way around touching all the points that stick out.

Then go back and trim out the little pieces with the tips of your scissors.

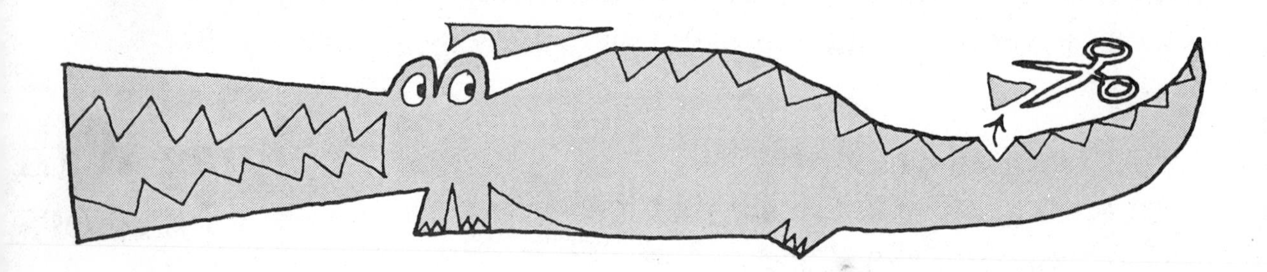

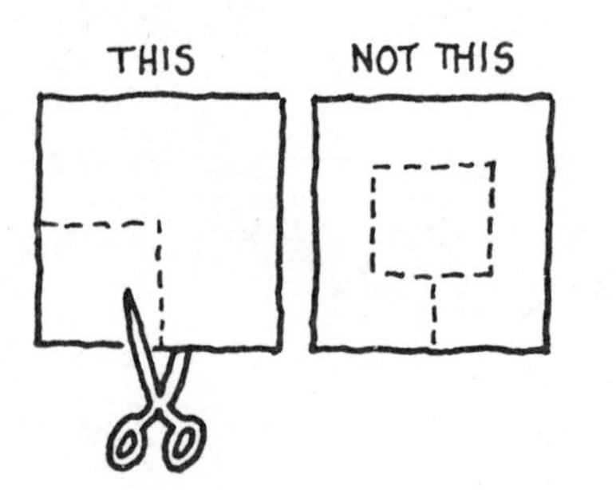

Cutting Two Edges to Get Four

When cutting a square or rectangle from a sheet of paper, cut it from one corner using two perfectly straight edges of the paper as two edges of your new shape.

Block Letters

To make letters that are all the same size for bulletin boards, posters, booklet covers, and so forth, first cut out paper rectangles all the same size. Then cut away pieces (shaded below) to create different letters and shapes.

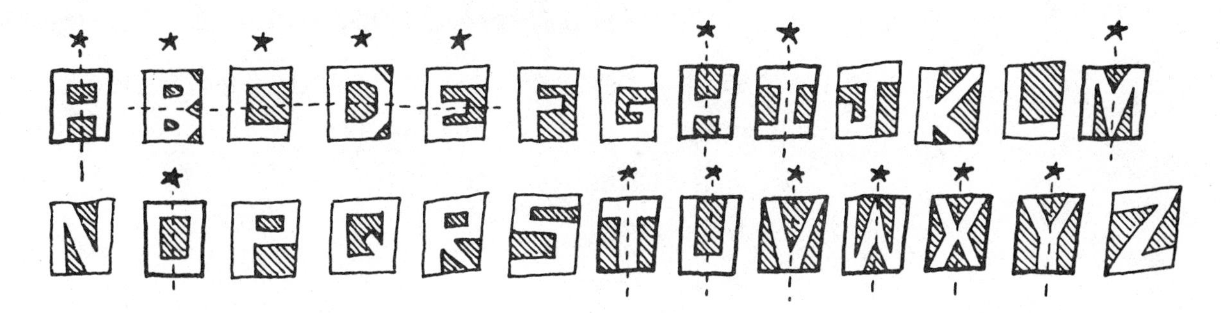

Symmetrical Shapes

The letters above shown with dotted lines through their centers are symmetrical—the same on both sides. Cutting perfectly symmetrical shapes is easy if you first fold the paper in half then cut out half the letter, heart, butterfly, or whatever.

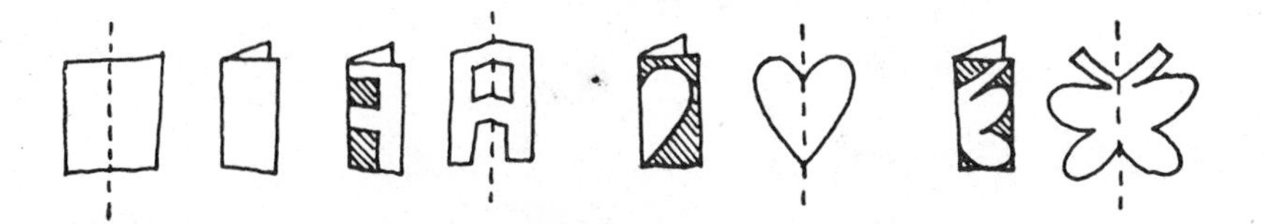

Decisions

Who Goes First?

When you and one other person need to decide who goes first at something, flip a coin. If you flip, your friend should call out "heads" or "tails" while the coin is in the air. If your friend calls out "heads" and the coin falls heads-up, he or she goes first; if it falls tails-up, you go first.

Decide who goes first in a group by figuring out whose birthday is coming up next. The next birthday after that goes second, and so on for the rest of the group.

Team Up

One way to divide a group into two teams is for everyone to stand side by side and count off. The first person in the line says "one", the next person says "two", then "one", then "two", and so on. All the people who said "one" become one team and the people who said "two" become the other.

One Divides, the Other Decides

When splitting something between two people, like the last piece of pie or cake, there will be no arguments if one person cuts the piece in two and the other gets first choice.

Old Tricks for a New Dog

A new puppy may cry at night because he's lonesome. Put a warm hot water bottle wrapped in a towel, a wind-up clock, or a small transistor radio in your puppy's bed. The warmth and soft noise will make him feel at home.

If your puppy runs away from you and doesn't come back when you call or whistle, instead of running after him try running in the other direction. Most puppies will turn and run after you. Fall down when the puppy gets close and most likely he will jump all over you.

This for That

When your dog has something that you want (like a ball or your sock), instead of trying to pull the thing away offer him something else (like a dog biscuit). Most times, the dog will drop the thing you want in favor of the new thing.

If you're outside, try throwing a stick and the dog might drop what you want and chase after the stick.

How to Stop a Dog Fight

Don't ever try to pull fighting dogs apart—you could get hurt. Instead, turn on the garden hose and distract the dogs from their squabble with a good soaking.

Dogs

Pedal On Past

When a dog starts chasing you while you're riding your bike, the best thing to do is look straight ahead and keep riding at a constant speed.

Introduce Yourself

When meeting a new dog speak to him softly and calmly and put your hand out, palm up, to let the dog sniff *before* you try to pet him.

Try not to make sudden movements around strange dogs or they may get frightened and bite you. Walk away from unfriendly animals. *Never run.*

Hot Dog!

Don't play too rough with your dog on hot days. Dogs don't know when to stop and may be overcome by the heat. Be sure your dog stays cool, and give him plenty of cool, fresh water.

H_2O UFO

On a picnic, a frisbee turned upside-down makes a good water dish for your dog.

Doggie Dessert

Your dog will love taking his heartworm pill or being brushed if you make a habit of giving him a treat immediately afterwards.

Dolls

Doll Dresses

Knee socks with no mates or ones with holes in the bottoms are just the right size for making clothes for fashion dolls.

Some baby dolls and teddy bears are big enough to wear hand-me-down clothes from a real baby.

Doll Tresses

Use an old toothbrush as a doll's hairbrush. The bristles are just the right size for small dolls.

A few drops of liquid fabric softener rubbed gently into a doll's hair will help the knots comb out.

Drawing

Mirror, Mirror, On the Wall

Learn to draw faces by drawing your own face while looking in a mirror.

A person's eyes are actually in the center of the head. To prove this, look in the mirror and put your index finger at the top of your nose (between your eyes) and your thumb on the bottom of your chin. Now hold this measurement steady and move your thumb to the position between your eyes: your index finger will line up with the top of your head.

The eyes are one eye's distance apart.

Drawing

Look Before You Draw

Artists say the key to realistic drawing is to spend more time looking than drawing. The real skill of drawing is not training your hand but learning to see the way things really look.

Before you put the first mark on paper, look at the thing you are about to draw for five full minutes.

Close Up and Far Away

There are four basic ways that an artist creates the illusion of depth in a picture:

1. **Size of objects.** Objects close up look larger than objects farther away. Things seem to get smaller as they move into the distance.
2. **Detail of objects.** Objects close up can be seen in greater detail than objects farther away. A tree seen from a distance is just a mass of green, but close up you can see individual leaves.
3. **Overlapping objects.** Objects close up often overlap, or partly cover up, objects farther away. If you can see all of something it's probably very close.
4. **Position on the page.** Objects close up are usually drawn closer to the bottom of the page than objects farther away. This is especially true of landscape pictures.

One Way? No Way!
Some people think there's only one way to draw a tree, one way to draw a house, one way to draw the sun . . . well, no way! There are as many ways to draw as there are people holding pencils. Look around you. You'll see that every tree and every house looks different and even the sun changes from noon to sunset. You're an artist, so find your own way.

Egg Dye

Glass cups are best for dyeing eggs. Use one glass for each color.

1. Fill a cup a little more than half-full with boiling water.
2. Add one teaspoon of white vinegar.
3. Add ten to twenty drops of food color.
4. Gently lower a hard-boiled egg into the dye with a spoon. Check often and remove the egg when you like its color.
5. Place the egg in a cardboard egg carton to dry.

*with an adult helper

Like Magic
Before dyeing a hard-boiled egg, draw designs on it with a white crayon. You won't see the crayon until you put the egg in dye; then your designs will magically appear. (Any light-colored crayon will do if you don't have white.)

Easter Eggs

The Golden Egg

Wait to dye the golden egg until you have dyed all the yellow eggs you want. Then add one or two drops of red food color to the yellow to make golden dye.

For orange dye use ten drops of yellow plus five drops or red.

For purple dye use nine drops of red plus three drops of blue.

Half-and-Half

Hold an egg halfway in dye for at least a minute. Remove and allow it to dry. Repeat, dyeing the other half a different color: a two-tone egg!

Egg Pocking

Before shelling Easter eggs to make egg salad or deviled eggs, here's one last game you can play with them. Each player starts out with an equal number of eggs. Two players, each holding one egg, face each other and roll their eggs to knock them together. If you crack the other player's egg without cracking your own, you get to keep the other player's cracked egg. If both eggs crack, each player keeps his or her own. The winner is the player who cracks the most eggs.

Emergency Know-How

Call the Police

In an emergency, if you don't know who to call first, call the police.

"O" for Operator

If you don't have the police phone number at the phone, dial "O" for operator. The operator will connect you to the nearest police station.

Don't Be the First to Hang Up

Let the person at the police station be the first to hang up. This way the police can get all the information they need and give you any instructions about what to do before they arrive.

Fears

Afraid of the Dark?

Try saying to yourself, "The nighttime is the same as the daytime, except there isn't as much light."

Calm Butterflies with X-Ray Vision

When you're getting up in front of a large group of people, and you're nervous, just picture them in their underwear!!!

Fears

Were You Ever Afraid?

Ask your parents and adult friends about their fears now and when they were kids. Hearing about their fears will probably make yours a little bit easier to handle. After all, *they* lived through it!

You're Not Alone

If you have particularly scary thoughts or something you're especially afraid of, tell your parent or an adult friend about it. Sometimes just telling someone else will make you feel better.

Football

Flag Football

Playing tackle football without wearing proper fitting equipment can be dangerous. For fun, play flag football instead. Each player sticks a flag (bandanna, handkerchief, or cloth napkin) in his or her back pocket. You "tackle" the player running with the ball by pulling the flag out of his pocket.

When playing with teams use flags of two different colors.

Open Target

Improve your aim by throwing a football through a hoop. Hang a hula hoop (or old tire) from a tree limb. Try to throw a football through the center as the hoop swings from side to side.

Nice Ice

Ice cubes don't have to be made of water. In an ice cube tray freeze your favorite fruit juice or soda pop to eat as a hot weather snack or add to a cold drink.

☐Freeze lemonade to serve in iced tea or juice.

☐Freeze chocolate milk to add flavor to a glass of plain milk.

☐Freeze fresh whole strawberries in ginger ale to add a fancy touch to any fruit drink.

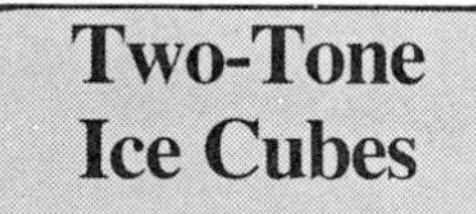

Two-Tone Ice Cubes

Your friends will be amazed.

1. Fill each compartment of an ice cube tray half-way with juice or soda pop.
2. Leave the tray in the freezer just until the top is frozen.
3. Fill the compartments the rest of the way with a different color beverage.
4. Let the cubes freeze for at least several hours before serving.

Freezer Treats

A-peeling Ice Pop
Freeze juice in a small cup for a no-mess summer treat. Just peel back the paper as you eat the ice pop.

Banana Manna
For an icy treat, peel a ripe banana, wrap it in plastic, and pop it in the freezer. If you like, stick a popsicle stick in one end before freezing.

Gifts

Good Gifts to Give and Get

- ☐ Tools for favorite activity
- ☐ Hobby equipment
- ☐ Art materials
- ☐ Scrapbooks or photo albums
- ☐ Additions to a collection
- ☐ Puzzle, riddle, or any kind of books
- ☐ A magazine subscription
- ☐ Tickets to some event (movie, game, or concert)
- ☐ A candlelight supper (or "dinner out")
- ☐ A framed photo of you (or drawing of you)
- ☐ Anything homemade (especially cookies)
- ☐ Personalized pencils, balloons, rubber stamps, bookplates, T-shirts, or anything with your friend's name printed on it!

Wrap Session

Look around your house for different sorts of paper to use as gift wrap: Sunday newspaper comic pages, old maps and posters, aluminum foil (space age gift wrap), colorful magazine pages for small gifts, and your own paintings and drawings that you don't mind cutting up and giving away.

Colorful paper napkins are dandy for wrapping up small treats or surprises (especially homemade cookies) for friends. Unfold and lay the napkin flat, put the treat in the center, pull up the four corners and tie it with a ribbon. Good for party favors too!

Use empty cardboard tubes as containers for small gifts. Roll gift wrap around the tube with about three inches of paper at each end. Gather and tie the ends closed with ribbon or yarn.

Disc Guises

A record album, even wrapped up in fancy paper, still looks like a record album. You can make it more of a surprise by using a gift wrap disguise:

Put the gift in a box that's bigger than it needs to be, then add a few lollipops. The rattle really throws 'em off.

Or crumble newspaper and tape it all over the plastic wrapped album—top, bottom, and sides so the album cover no longer appears square. Then wrap it up loosely or put it in a bag. Who ever heard of a soft, bumpy record album?

Glitter

Sparkle Wrap

With white glue clearly write a simple message or the receiver's name on top of a wrapped-up present, then sprinkle on glitter.

Save Glitter

Before glittering anything fold a large piece of paper in half then unfold and place underneath to catch extra glitter. After gently shaking loose glitter onto the paper, fold in half again and pour the glitter back into its container.

Glue

Rubber Cement

When neatness is important (for example, when you're making a poster or report cover) use rubber cement. Brush the glue onto both surfaces, let dry, then slowly and carefully put the cutout into place. (Once the two surfaces touch they're stuck for good so *be careful.*) Extra glue around the edges can be rubbed off with a clean fingertip.

Glue

White Glue
When gluing a cut out shape to another piece of paper, put little dots of glue all around the edge of the cutout (on the back, of course). Just before you turn the cutout over to glue it down, spread the dots of glue by quickly moving your fingertip all the way around the edge of the shape.

No glue squishes out to mess up your art work.

Wheat Paste
If you run out of white glue, mix up your own wheat paste. It works very well for gluing paper together. Just put some white flour in a bowl and add a little water at a time, mixing with your fingers until the wheat paste is slightly thinner than mashed potatoes.

Goldfish

Only Use Settled Water
Never run tap water directly into your goldfish bowl. Let water settle in a pitcher or other container for at least twenty-four hours. As the water settles, it reaches room temperature and harmful gasses escape.

Goldfish

Goldfish Mathematics

Remember this rule to decide how big a bowl your goldfish need:

the number of *inches* of goldfish (not counting tails) = the number of *gallons* of water.

If you have trouble measuring gallons, remember that 1 gallon equals four quarts or 16 cups.

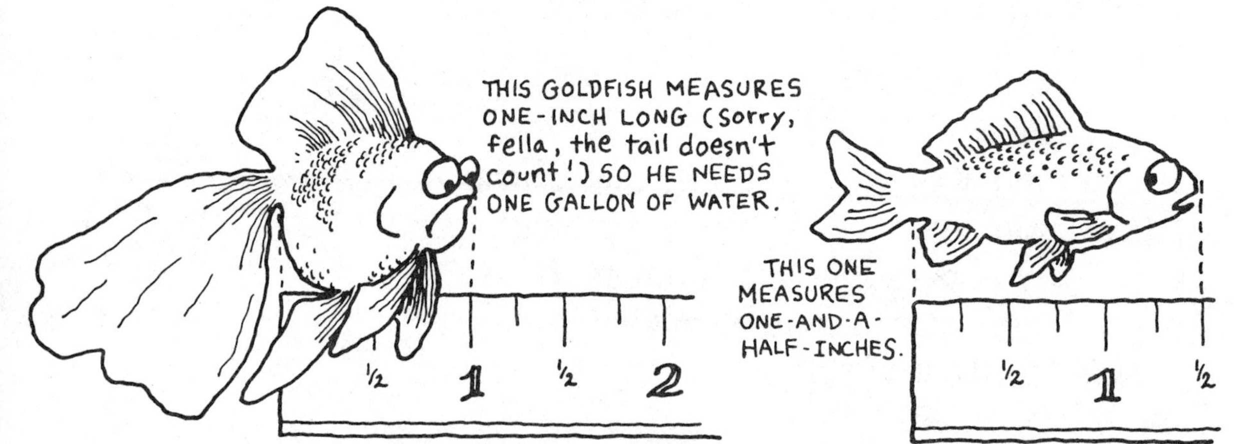

Change the Water

Every two weeks, take out half of the water in the goldfish bowl (but not the fish) and replace it with settled water.

Pour in settled water only to the widest part of the goldfish bowl to make sure your fish get plenty of oxygen.

THIS

NOT THIS

Home Sweet Home

When you bring home a new fish in a plastic bag, float the bag in the goldfish bowl for at least fifteen minutes to let the water temperature in the bag and bowl become the same. Then let the fish out of the bag into its new home.

What Nets Are For

Never touch goldfish. Your fingers might rub off the film that protects their scales.

Change of Diet

If you run out of fish food, you can substitute a small pinch of ground up dog biscuit, oatmeal, or cornmeal. You can even feed your fish a tiny piece of lettuce or cooked potato, but *never more than a tiny pinch* of anything.

Who Wants Leftovers?

Clean your goldfish bowl of leftover food with a clear plastic drinking straw. Capture the food inside the straw, place your finger over the end to hold it in, then empty the food into the trash by removing your finger.

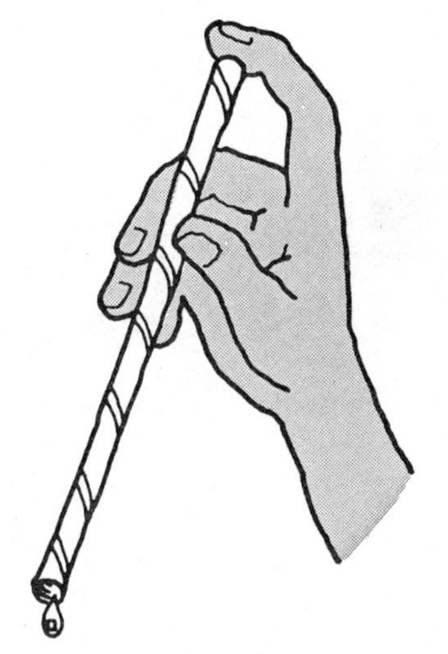

Hair

Rinse and Shine

If you leave any shampoo in your hair it won't look shiny. After rinsing pull a few strands of wet hair through your fingers. If your hair squeaks all the shampoo is out. (If not, keep rinsing.)

Rinse your hair in cold water to make it shine even more. (A cold water rinse also makes curly hair less frizzy.)

Your great-grandmother probably knew this tip for shinier hair: after shampooing rinse with a little vinegar (for dark hair) or lemon juice (for blond or red hair). Then rinse with clear water.

Wait Till It Dries

To prevent your hair from breaking or splitting, never pin, tie, or braid your hair when it is wet. Wet hair is very stretchy and if it is pulled tightly, it will break when it dries.

Halloween Costumes

Who Is That?!

Change your body shape or height. Stuff your costume with crumpled newspaper or pillows, or wear an oversized mask and hat.

Disguise your hands too. Make them up to match your face or simply wear gloves. (For monster hands staple cardboard claws on work gloves . . . before you put them on!)

Halloween Costumes

Off to a Good Start

When you set out to make a costume, start with an overall body costume as a base.

- ☐ Large cardboard box (robots, mailboxes, skyscrapers, and such)
- ☐ Pillowcase, with arm and neck holes (tie at waist for Roman togas, stuff for monster bodies or giant marshmallows)
- ☐ Sheet (Boo!)
- ☐ Leotard and tights, or . . .
- ☐ One-piece pajamas (add tail, wings, and so forth for animals and extra-terrestrials)
- ☐ Old clothes (witches, hobos, scarecrows, and such—look around your house or try a thrift shop).

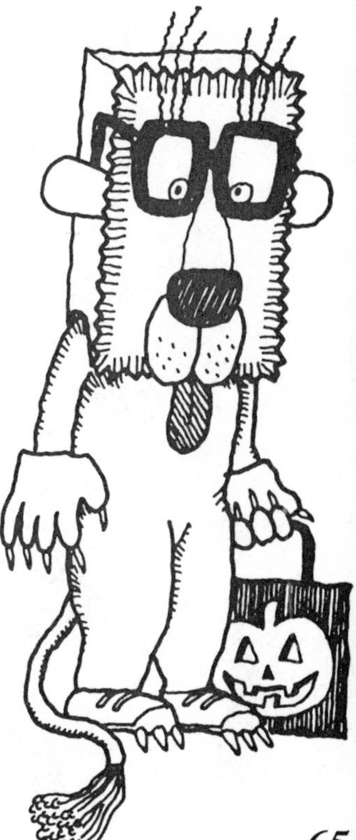

Wacky Wig

Tape long locks (of yarn or ribbon) to the inside brim of a hat. Use wide masking or duct tape.

Play It Safe

Design a light colored costume or add reflective tape so you'll be easily seen in the dark.

Also, never go near any flame with a costume on.

Halloween Costumes

What's a Go Non?!

If people ask, "What are you?" and you don't have a name for your Halloween costume, just say you're a Go Non.

Halloween Makeup

Mask or Makeup?

Your choice! A mask goes on quickly and completely hides your face but may be uncomfortable and keep you from seeing well.

Makeup takes longer to put on but leaves your face free so you can see clearly and eat and drink easily.

Blue Faces and Red Noses

Different shades of eyeshadow and lipstick can be used for color anywhere on your face. (But never use someone's makeup without asking first.)

Vampire Blood

For realistic-looking blood, stir a few drops of red food coloring into some raw egg white.

Get Old Fast
To turn your hair gray, pat baby powder all over it.

Halloween Greasepaint

This homemade makeup wipes off easily with tissue.

1. Put one tablespoon of cold cream in a small dish.
2. Stir in two teaspoons of cornstarch.
3. Add a teaspoon of water.
4. Add a few drops of food color and stir well.

Be Whiskered
Stick paper or cotton beards to your face with corn syrup.

For a scruffy beard, first rub on some corn syrup then pat on dry coffee grounds.

A Cure for the Hiccups
Swallow nine times.

Hopscotch

Rainy Day Hopscotch

Use thin masking tape to lay out an indoor hopscotch court on tile or low-pile carpet in your room.

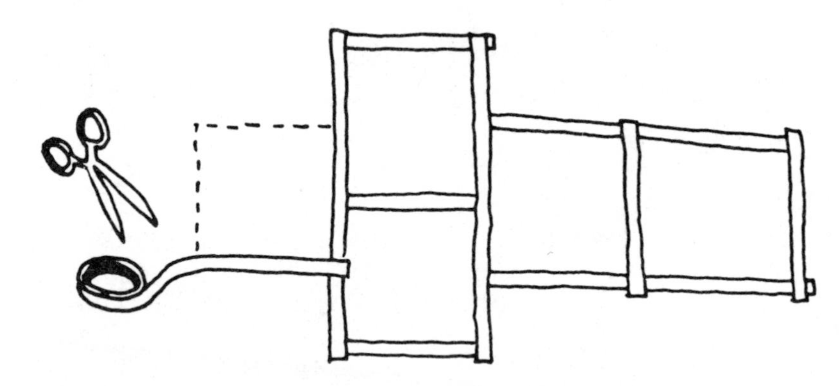

Horses

Stay in Front

When walking from one side of a horse to the other, walk around his head so he can keep his eye on you and cannot kick you. If you must walk behind him, pat him gently on his thigh to let him know you're there.

Lead from the Left

Almost all horses are used to being led and mounted from their left side.

Good Grooming

When grooming a horse (or any animal), always brush in the direction his hair grows. Look carefully to find the many changes of direction in hair growth.

Hospital

It's No Vacation, But . . .
A short stay in the hospital won't be too bad if you make friends there. Start by learning the names of the nurses and doctors who'll be taking care of you.

Ask Questions
When something seems scary (at the hospital or doctor's office) ask questions. Frightening-looking things don't seem so scary when you know what they are and what they are for.

Hot Pepper

Hot Tamales Too Hot?
If you take a bite of food that is too spicy hot, cool off your mouth by immediately eating some plain bread. This works much better than drinking water.

Hot Weather

Be Cool
To cool off quickly, run some cold tap water over the inside of your wrists.

Hot Weather

Cool as a Cowboy

A cool trick cowboys have for beating the heat is to soak bandannas in cold water, wring them out, and put them on top of their heads. They look silly, but they feel cool.

Cool Colors

Wearing light colored clothes keeps you cooler on a hot day. Light colors reflect the heat, while dark colors absorb it.

Chores to Volunteer For

When it's just too hot to do *anything,* volunteer to help clean out the refrigerator or defrost the freezer.

Keep cool and make some money at the same time—wash cars or water gardens. Wear your bathing suit so you can get wet . . . "by accident".

Or put on your bathing suit and give your dirty dog a bath outdoors.

House Numbers

When Looking for a House Number

Usually odd numbers (3, 5, 7, etc.) are on one side of the street and even numbers (2, 4, 6, etc.) are on the other. See if house numbers are getting greater or lesser to figure out if you're headed in the right direction.

How Do You Do's

Nice to Meet You

To introduce your mother or father to your teacher, say your teacher's name first.

To introduce *yourself* to someone, just say, "Hi. My name is ________________."

Ice Cream

Hard to Dish Out

If your ice cream is frozen too hard, just dip your spoon in warm water between each scoop.

Dusty Sundae

Sprinkle chocolate milk mix or instant malted milk powder on top of ice cream for a speedy, special sundae.

Itches

Scratch Somewhere Else

If you're itchy somewhere you can't scratch, scratch another spot. It helps.

Jack-O'-Lanterns

Carve a Star

Whoever gets this job in your family knows the first step of carving a jack-o'lantern is to cut the top out of the pumpkin, remove it, and scoop out the seeds. Instead of just cutting a circle, carve a zig-zag line around the stem. The resulting star shaped lid is great looking and fits back in perfectly.

Slant the knife blade in toward the center of the pumpkin as you cut so the lid won't fall inside.

Roasted Pumpkin Seeds

Remember this trick for a treat.

1. Heat oven to 350ºF.
2. With a big metal spoon, scoop out the seeds from a pumpkin.
3. In a bowl of water separate the seeds from the strings and pulp.
4. Spread the seeds on a cookie sheet.
5. Sprinkle with a little corn oil and salt.
6. Bake for about 15 minutes.

Jewelry

Easy Off

If a ring gets stuck on your finger, rub some baby oil or soap suds all over the ring and finger and you should be able to slide it off.

Tangle Free

To keep a chain from tangling, always hook it closed again as soon as you take it off.

Button Hold

To keep pierced earrings together, fasten them through two holes of a small button, then put the button in a safe place.

Chalk-in-the-Box

A piece of chalk in your jewelry box will keep most costume jewelry from tarnishing.

Jigsaw Puzzles

Portable Puzzle

If you have a big piece of plywood, pegboard, heavy cardboard, or anything large and flat, use it as a surface on which to put together your jigsaw puzzle. You can move it around easily and store it under your bed when you're not working on the puzzle.

To find what size surface you need, look on the box to see how big the finished puzzle will be.

Jigsaw Puzzles

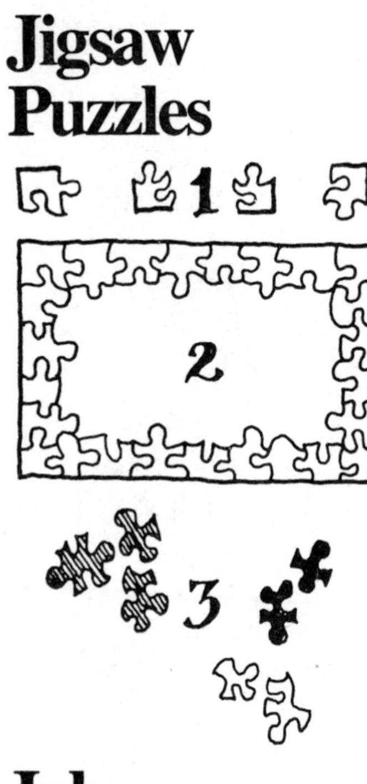

How to Start a Jigsaw Puzzle

1. Find the four corner pieces.
2. Find all the straight-edged pieces and put together the frame.
3. Separate the pieces by different colors and work on one colored section at a time.

Jigsaw Puzzlers Unite

After you've done a jigsaw puzzle trade it for a puzzle someone else has already done.

Many public libraries loan jigsaw puzzles. Ask your librarian.

Jobs

Products and Services

Basically there are two ways to make money:

1. You can perform a service (such as baby-sitting, dog walking, firewood stacking, snow shoveling, lawn mowing, or window washing).
2. You can sell a product (home-baked cookies, lemonade, home-grown vegetables, wild berries, houseplants from cuttings, crafts, or toys).

Jobs

Choosing a Job

To think of a way to make money, start by thinking of what you really like to do. If you like pets, perhaps you could walk your neighbors' dogs. If you like flowers, maybe you could grow zinnias to sell in summer bouquets.

Advertise!

Make your own business cards to attract new customers. Give them to people you know. Ask your parents to give some out too.

Jump Rope

The Tree Makes Three

If you have only one other person to play with, tie one end of the jump rope to a tree.

Ketchup

No Flow?

Push a clean drinking straw to the bottom of a bottle of stubborn ketchup. (Wait, don't drink it!!) Pull out the straw and the ketchup will pour out easily.

When you get near the bottom of the bottle add a teaspoon of water to the ketchup, put the cap on and shake it up. The last of the ketchup will flow out a little easier.

Keys

Four Ways to Hold On to Your Key

1. Wear the key on a chain or cord around your neck.
2. Put it on a key ring and attach the ring to the pull of your coat zipper.
3. Attach the key ring to your belt loop.
4. Thread the key onto your shoelace (between the eyelets so it can't slip off if your shoe comes untied).

In the Bag

If you carry a bag or knapsack you'll locate your key quickly if the key chain is attached to something big, bright, and clunky like a wiffle ball or a toy character.

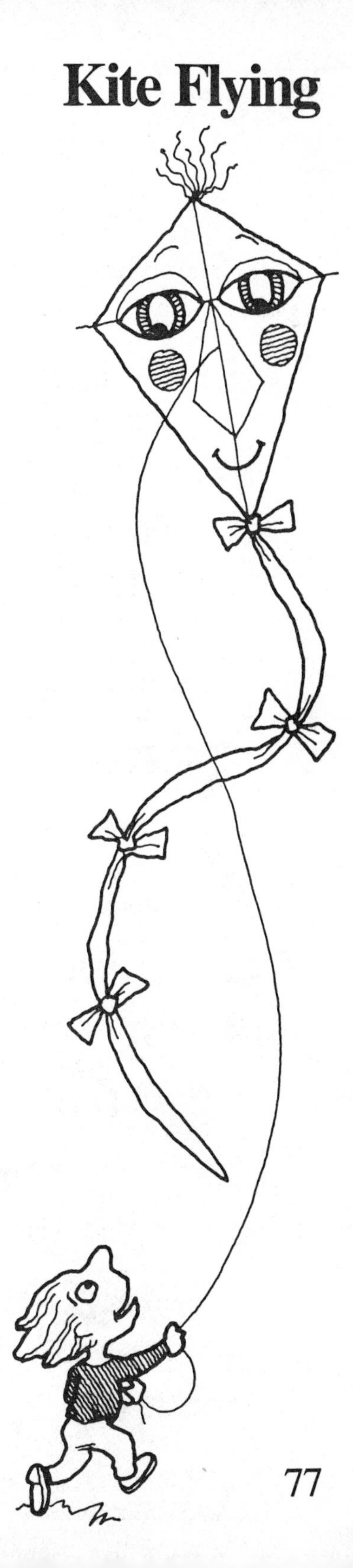

Perfect Wind

When you can hear leaves rustling, the wind is perfect for kite flying.

Don't Let Go

To make a kite climb higher, let the line go loose, then quickly pull it tight again.

This Tail's a Long One

A kite tail should be long and light, not short and heavy. The harder the wind, the longer the tail needs to be.

Tail Materials

To make a tail for your kite, cut strips about thirty inches long and two inches wide from an old sheet, crepe paper streamers, or a plastic trash bag. Tie the ends of the strips together.

Knots

Best Knot to Know

The square knot is the most often-used knot. It suits many purposes, holds tightly, and is as easy to untie as it is to tie. When you tie the square knot remember the phrase, "Left over right, right over left."

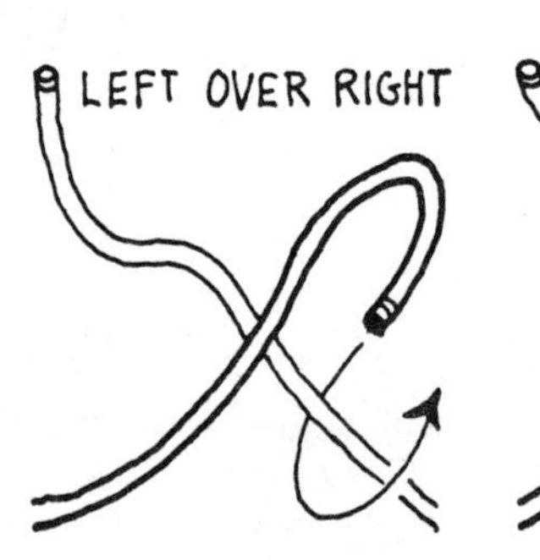

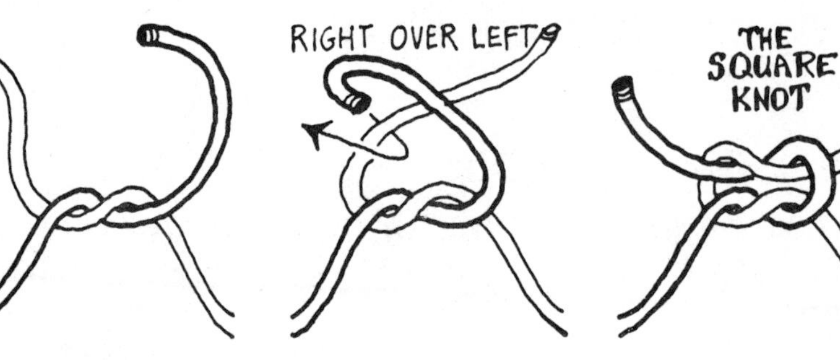

Granny Knot

You may tie a "granny knot" by mistake if you forget "Left over right, right over left." Just untie it and try again.

Lemonade Stands

Real Lemonade

All you need is lemons, sugar, and water.

1. In a large glass stir 1 cup of water and 3 teaspoons of sugar.
2. Stir in the juice of a half lemon (2 to 4 tablespoons).
3. Add a few ice cubes.

Add thin slices of lemon to the glass to make it pretty.

Lemonade Stands

Made with Real Lemons

Your lemonade will be the best on the block if you add some real lemon juice to a pitcher of lemonade made from a mix or concentrate.

Step Right Up

Make a big, colorful sign to say what you're selling and how much it costs.

Second Thirst

Sometimes, if you offer customers a salty snack like potato chips, they'll buy another glass of lemonade.

Mobile Lemonade

If you're not getting many customers at your lemonade stand, maybe you're standing in the wrong spot. Try putting everything from the stand into a wagon and wheeling it around to find customers.

Lifting Heavy Things

Don't Strain

Always crouch down to pick something up from the ground—this way your leg muscles do a lot of the work.

People often hurt themselves by picking up things that are too heavy. Don't take a chance: if something feels too heavy, ask someone to help.

Lightning

Lay Low
If you are caught outdoors in a thunderstorm, keep low and away from tall trees or any other object that sticks high into the air. Lightning usually strikes the tallest thing around; for heaven's sake, don't *be* the tallest thing around.

Never swim during a thunderstorm.

Metal attracts lightning. Do not hold anything made of metal or be near it during a thunderstorm. However, if you are in a closed metal car, you are perfectly safe.

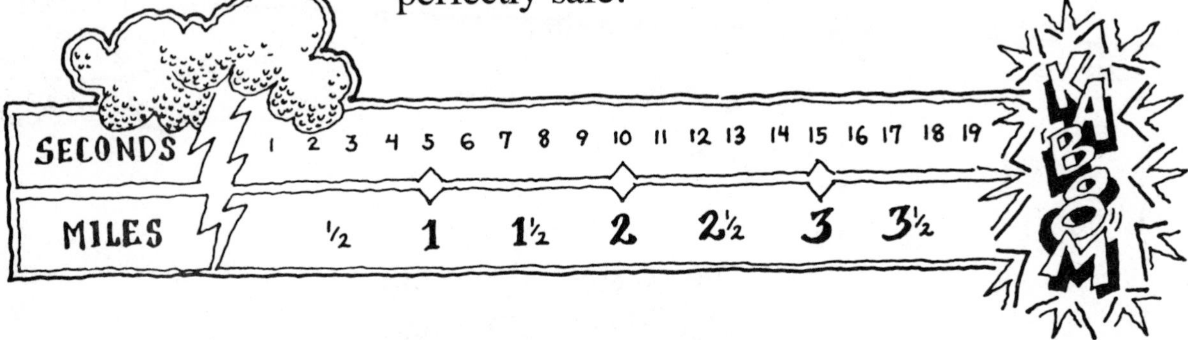

Flash . . . Kaboom!
To figure how far away a storm is, watch for a flash of lightning then count off seconds until you hear thunder. Thunder travels one mile in five seconds so if you count to five before you hear thunder, the storm is about one mile away. If you count to ten, it is two miles away. (The reason you see the lightning before you hear the thunder is that light travels much faster than sound.)

Lightning

Count Off Seconds

If you don't have a watch with a second hand, count off seconds this way: one-one-thousand, two-one-thousand, three-one-thousand, four-one-thousand, and so on. (Saying each number plus "one-thousand" takes about one second.)

Loosening Lids

Open Up!

If the lid of a jar or bottle is too tight to unscrew, turn the container upside-down and tap the lid once, gently but firmly, on a hard surface (such as a countertop). If the lid still doesn't unscrew, run hot tap water over it for about fifteen seconds then try again.

Lost In A Crowd

Rendezvous

When you go to a place where you could get separated from your companions (like a fair or a large shopping center), agree when you first get there on a place to meet in case somebody gets lost.

Who Will Help?

If you're lost and need help, the best person to ask is a police officer. If you don't see one, you could also ask another community helper like a mailman, bus driver, storekeeper, or someone at an information desk. An adult with a child will usually be willing to help you out, too.

Lost In The Woods

Stay Put

If you ever get separated from a group on a camping trip or hike in the woods, stay where you are and let your companions search for *you*.

Just Whistle

Carry along a whistle when you head for the woods. If you should become lost, blow it sharply three times and repeat this pattern every few minutes. Any kind of signal repeated three times at frequent intervals is a universal distress call and should bring help.

Lunchboxes

Inside Information

A magnet is great for attaching a dollar bill or important notes to the inside cover of your metal lunchbox.

Lunchboxes

Cupcake Sandwich

If you unwrap your cupcake for dessert, and more frosting sticks to the waxed paper than to the cupcake, here's a tip for you. Before wrapping, cut the cupcake through the center and put the top half, upside-down, onto the bottom half so the frosting is in the middle. Only the frosting that squishes out the sides will stick to the wrapping.

Recycle!

Don't throw away last year's lunchbox. It makes a good portable storage box for small toys, art supplies, puzzles, and so forth.

Magnifying Glasses

Explore!

Explore a small part of a garden, park, or your own backyard with a magnifying glass. Look carefully at bugs, flowers, leaves, grass, soil, and especially under and inside things. You'll be amazed at the tiny creatures and details you have never seen.

If you don't have a magnifying glass, fill a small zip-lock plastic bag with water to make a magnifier to use outdoors.

Making Copies

Carbon Copies

If you think ahead, you can make a copy of any drawing, letter, homework assignment, or other pen or pencil work by simply putting a piece of carbon paper, inky side down, between two sheets of plain paper. As you write or draw on the top sheet, the carbon paper makes an exact copy on the sheet beneath.

You can buy carbon paper at almost any dime store or pharmacy.

Instant Copies

Next time you need a black and white copy of a picture from a book to use in a report booklet, or want to make a copy of that test you aced to send to your grandma, think of instant copy machines. You'll find one in almost every public library and post office.

Medicine

Yuk!

If you must take bad tasting medicine:

Suck on an ice cube first—the cold will numb your taste buds. (Or suck on a menthol cough drop.)

Or, hold your nose while you're taking the medicine, then drink something you like.

Here's How to Remember . . .
The order of the colors in a rainbow:

Remember the name, "ROY G. BIV".

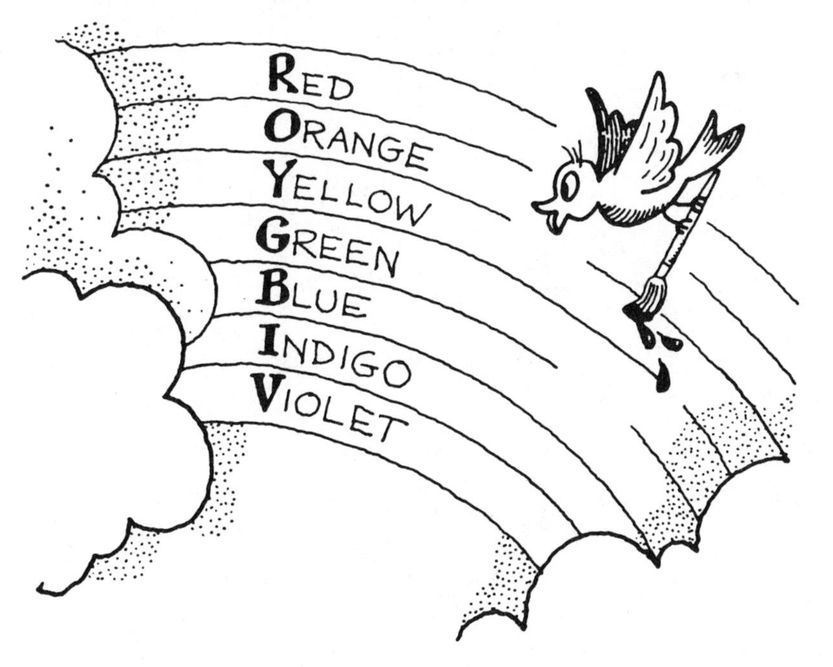

The order of the Great Lakes (from west to east):

Remember the silly sentence, "Sally made Harry eat onions."

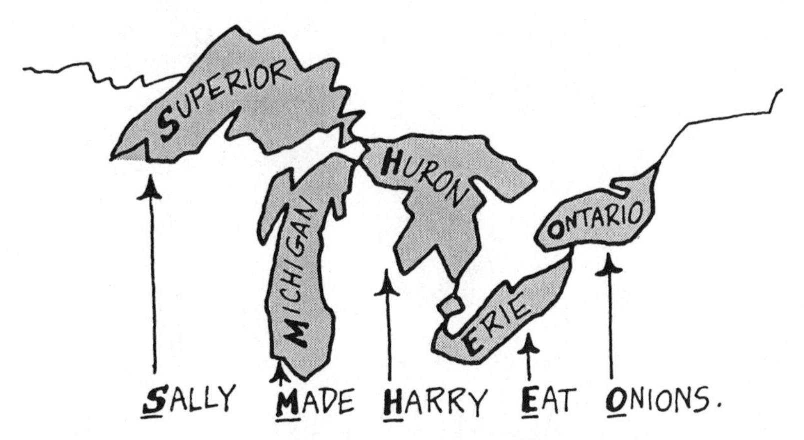

Memory Devices

The order of the planets (from the sun):

Remember the silly sentence, "My very educated mother just served us nine pizzas."

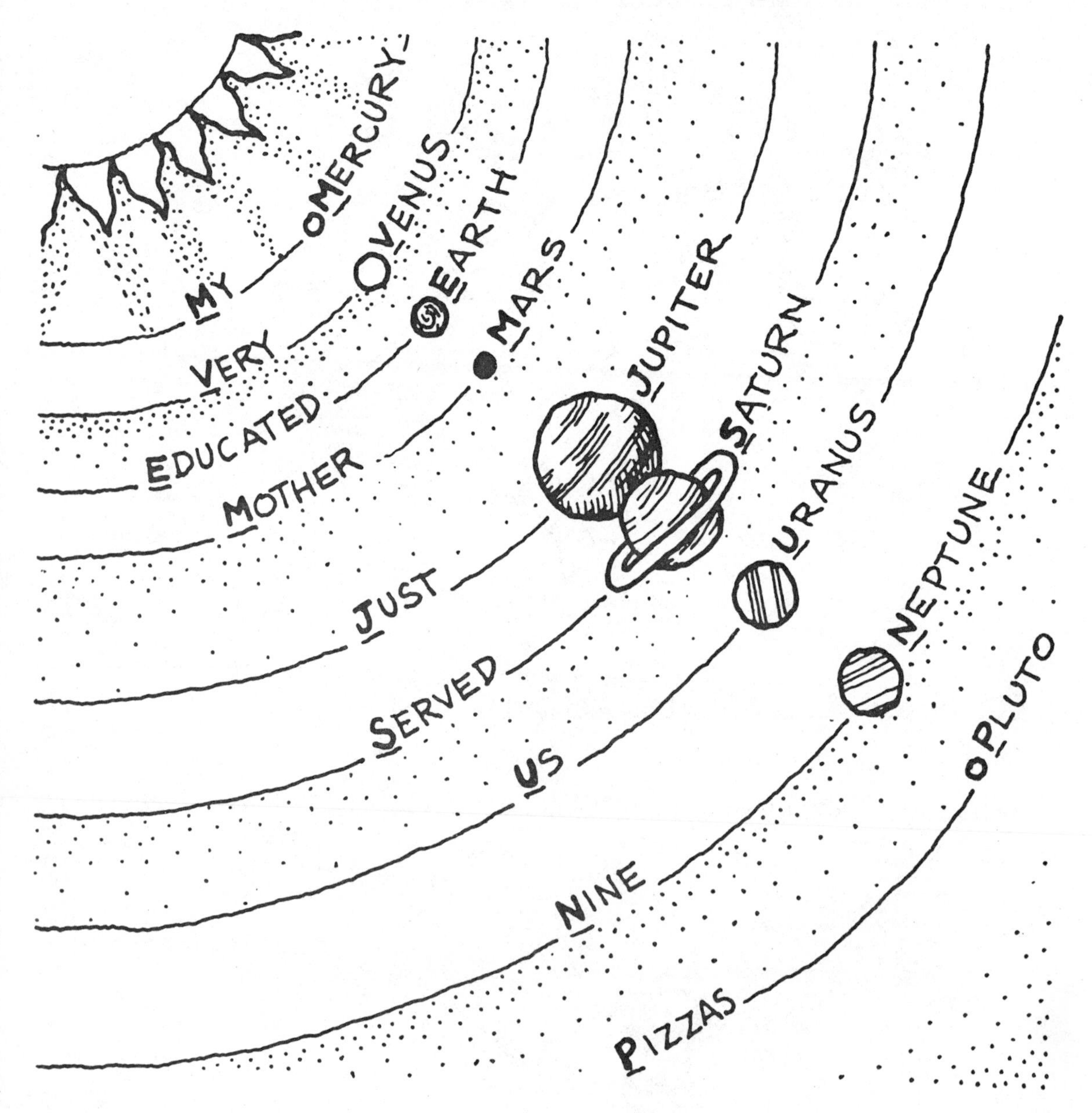

Which months have 31 days:

Make a fist. With the first finger of your other hand touch the knuckles and valleys between the knuckles in the following order, saying the names of the months as you go . . .

All the months "on knuckles" have 31 days. All the months "in valleys" have 30 days, except for February with *28* (or *29* in a leap year).

Milk Drinks

Milk Shook

You don't need ice cream to make a milk shake.

1. Pour one cup of very cold milk in a blender or in a clean glass jar with a screw top.
2. Add two teaspoons of sugar and one quarter teaspoon of vanilla.
3. Whir it in the blender or shake it up in the tightly covered jar.

Soda Jerks' Secret

The secret for making "fluffy" milk shakes is using very cold milk.

Missing Pieces

Write for Replacements

If you lose an important piece to a game, puzzle, or toy, write the company that made it and very clearly describe what you lost. Often companies will replace missing pieces free of charge or at a small cost.

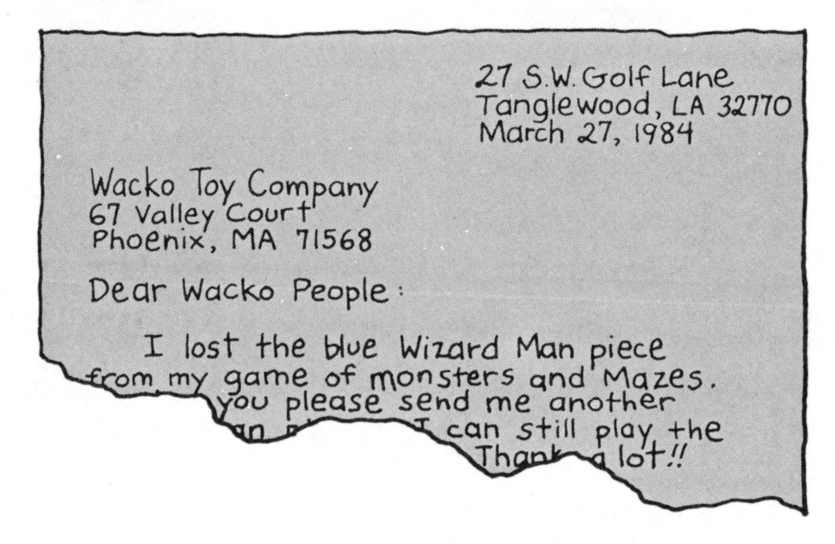

27 S.W. Golf Lane
Tanglewood, LA 32770
March 27, 1984

Wacko Toy Company
67 Valley Court
Phoenix, MA 71568

Dear Wacko People:

I lost the blue Wizard Man piece
from my game of monsters and Mazes.
you please send me another
I can still play the
Thank a lot!!

Mittens

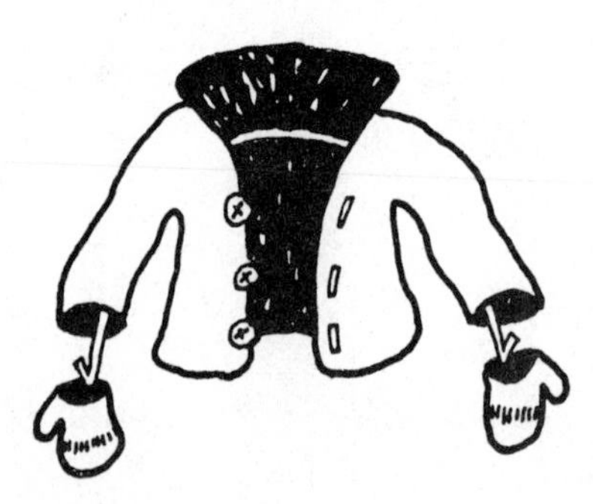

Hold On To Your Mittens

If you ever lose your mittens or gloves (who doesn't?) try this trick for keeping your winter coat and mittens together: Draw a long piece of string up through one sleeve and down through the other. Fasten the string ends to your mittens with safety pins or needle and thread. When you take the mittens off they'll still hang around, and when you put on your coat again they'll always be there.

Finger Tip

Fingers stay warmer in mittens than in gloves. In mittens warm air can move all around the fingers and there's less surface area exposed to the cold.

Terrific with a Capital T

With your brothers and sisters buy a T-shirt (or sweatshirt) that says "World's Greatest Mom". You can choose the shirt color and the style of letters you want at lots of T-shirt and novelty stores.

(Don't forget "World's Greatest Dad" on Father's Day.)

Mother's Day Outing

Take your mom on a very special picnic. You and Dad pack the lunch basket. Include her favorite sandwiches and some little wrapped-up surprise. Give Mom a kite for a present, then help her fly it.

Funny Family Portrait

Draw a cartoon picture of your whole family doing things they really do around your house. Exaggerate everything to make it funny. Frame it or put it on page one of a brand new scrapbook for your mom.

Surprise!

To really surprise your mother, wrap up your present to her, sneak out and put it by your front door, ring the doorbell and hide.

Motion Sickness

Carsick

To prevent carsickness, try sitting in the front seat. It's less bumpy and you get a better view.

Avoid reading in the car or staring at the road out of a side window. Instead, play some of the travel games suggested under travel pastimes—or any others you can think up.

If you do start feeling carsick, roll down the window a little to let some fresh air blow on your face.

Or, if there's room, lie flat in the back seat and go to sleep.

Seasick

If you start to feel seasick, go on deck in the fresh air and watch the shore, birds, other boats—anything except the waves.

Muscles

Calf Stretch

After a hike, long bike ride, or other exercise that makes your legs ache, put one foot about ten inches directly in front of the other. Lean forward as far as you can without lifting your back heel from the floor. Reverse feet and do it again. This stretches the calf muscles and will make them feel better.

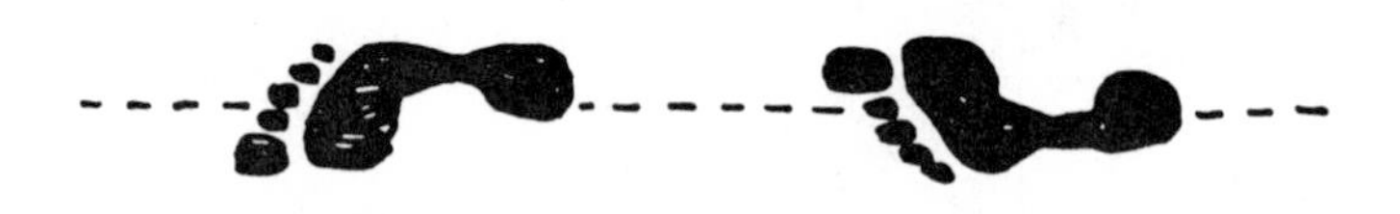

Warm Up

It's important to warm up your muscles before putting them to work. Always start off vigorous sports and games slowly with gentle exercise and stretching.

Warm Down

Avoid stiff muscles by bundling up after vigorous exercise. (A sweat suit fits this purpose well.)

Two Ways to Relieve Aching Muscles

Take a warm bath.

Sleep in a sleeping bag.

Nosebleeds

To Stop a Nosebleed

Keep your head in a normal position and hold your nose firmly in the center, pinching it closed for at least five minutes.

Overnight Parties

Anticipation

A long party will be more fun if there's something special to look forward to. Plan a snack or an activity for a certain time ("Popcorn at ten" or "Ghost stories at eleven") and let your guests know what fun is on the way.

Overnight Parties

Penalties and Fortunes

Before your sleepover party write some funny "penalties" on small pieces of paper, roll them up, and put them inside balloons. Penalties are messages such as "Make believe you are eating a worm" or "Act like a monkey". During the party each guest must pop one balloon and do what the note says. (Don't write any penalties that you wouldn't do yourself.)

Or put "fortunes" in the balloons: "You will be a famous soccer player" and "You will have seven children" and so forth.

Boo!

A few days before your sleepover party, check out some ghost stories from the library. Choose a few stories to tell once the evening gets dark and quiet.

To really surprise your guests, arrange beforehand to have someone in your family knock on the wall or window, or turn out the lights, while you're telling ghost stories. Guaranteed to make everyone scream!

Overnight Parties

Sign In Please

An autograph book (or a stuffed toy made for autographing) makes a good gift if you're going to an overnight birthday party.

Packing

Packing for a Trip

Whether for overnight or longer, when you're checking to make sure you've packed everything use this trick: Think over what you need from your feet up.

Once you get to the top of your head, imagine what you'll be doing each day of your trip from the time you get up in the morning till the time you go to bed. This will help you think of the things you need to take other than clothes and grooming supplies.

Address Ahead

Before you take off for summer camp or a vacation, think of all the people to whom you'll send letters—your parents, grandparents and friends. Stamp and address envelopes to them ahead of time and pack them along with your stationery and pen. Then, on your trip, all you have to do is write the letters—no searching for addresses and stamps.

Packing

Don't Forget Plastic Bags

Use them to pack shoes, shampoo bottles, dirty clothes, and anything else you want to keep separate from other things in your suitcase.

Painting

Experiment!

There are many tools other than paintbrushes that can be used to apply paint and create different effects: fingers, hands, sponges, cotton swabs, cotton balls, crumpled paper, old toothbrushes (rub them for a spatter effect), twigs, feathers, and other natural objects.

Primitive Paintbrush

If you don't have a paintbrush, make your own. Pound the end of a twig, turning it as you hammer, until it frays into many thin fibers like the bristles of a brush.

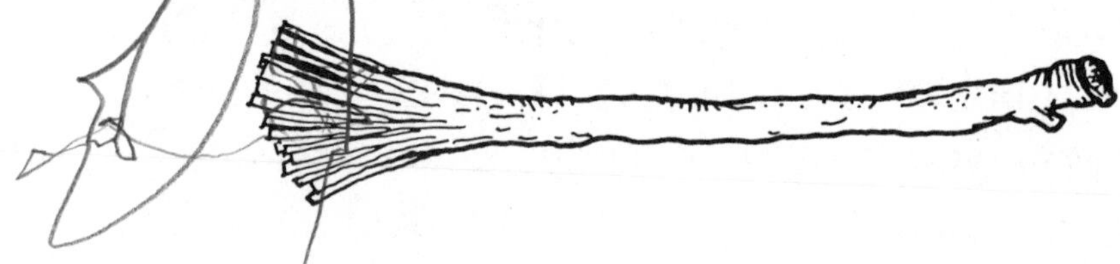

The Wet Look

For a really special effect, try painting (or drawing with chalk or felt-tip water color pens) on wet paper.

Stick to It

To get water paint to stick to glass or shiny paper, add a few drops of dishwashing liquid.

Painting

Brush Up on Your Technique

Paint should be thick enough to stay on the brush but thin enough to flow easily from the brush onto the paper. Thin down water paint by adding a little water. Thin down oil paint by adding a few drops of oil or paint thinner.

Dip your brush in paint often but only halfway up the bristles. You have more control over where the paint goes, and cleanup is much easier afterwards.

Never grind a brush onto paper to "get out more paint"—this just breaks the bristles and ruins the brush. Instead, dip the brush again each time it begins to run out of paint.

Always clean a paintbrush as soon as you finish using it. Store clean brushes, bristles up, in a jar or can.

Paper Folding

Make a Square

Paper folding projects often require a square to begin with, but you may only have a rectangular sheet of paper. What to do? Fold the paper diagonally so its top edge touches one side. Then neatly cut off the part that sticks out at the bottom.

Paper Folding

Fold a Paper Cup

Once you learn this paper folding trick, you'll never be without a paper cup (if you have a clean piece of plain paper, that is).

Fold a paper square in half on the diagonal. (Step 1 & 2)

Fold the right corner up to touch the left side of the triangle, so it looks about like this. (Step 3 & 4)

Fold the left corner up, too. (Step 5 & 6)

Now there are two little triangles sticking out the top. Fold the front one forward and the rear one back. (Step 7, 8 & 9)

Push the top corners toward each other to open the cup. Fill and drink. (Step 10 & 11)

Nifty Napkins

Here's a fancy way to fold paper napkins for a party or special dinner.

Unfold each napkin to make a long rectangle, then pleat or accordian-fold the whole thing. Slip it into a napkin ring (or tie it with a ribbon) then pull at the top and bottom to make it fan out.

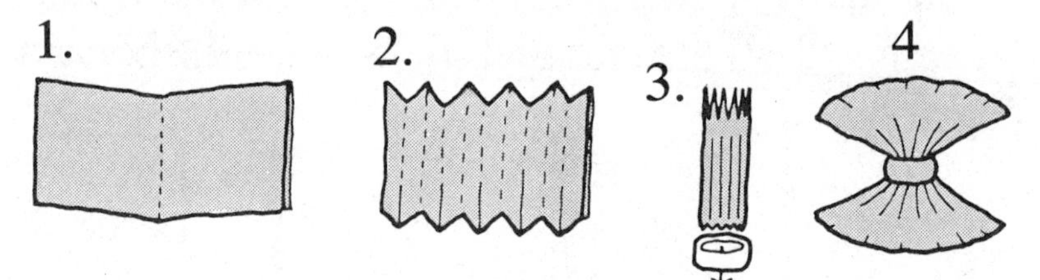

Paper For Projects

Free for the Asking

There are probably several places in your community where you can get extra paper for drawing, painting, construction, and collage projects.

- ☐ Local newspaper office (Ask for extra newsprint.)
- ☐ Printer (Ask for throwaway paper.)
- ☐ Business offices (Ask for throwaway paper printed on only one side or computer printouts.)
- ☐ School office (Ask for misprinted mimeos.)
- ☐ Wallpaper store (Ask for out-of-date wallpaper sample books: fancy patterned paper!)
- ☐ You may have extra paper bags and shirt cardboards in your own home.

Peanut Butter

How to Keep the Peanut Butter Out of the Jelly Jar

1. Always spread the jelly side first.
2. Wipe the knife clean on the other piece of bread.
3. Spread the peanut butter.

When to Put the Jelly In the Peanut Butter Jar

Peanut butter and jelly can be mixed in one jar to save room when packing for a camping trip.

Peanut Butter

A Toast to Peanut Butter

A peanut butter and jelly sandwich made in the morning can get pretty soggy by lunchtime. For an unsoggy sandwich, toast the bread first.

A Honey of a Tip

If you buy "natural" peanut butter, add one or two tablespoons of honey the first time you stir it up. This keeps the oil from coming to the top and tastes great too.

Pencils And Erasers

1, 2, 3, 4, Here's What the Numbers Are

Pencils are often marked 1, 2, 3, 4, or H to indicate the hardness of the pencil lead.

Soft pencils write dark, smudge easily, but are very good for drawing. They must be sharpened often.

Hard pencils make a light, thin line, don't smudge and last longer between sharpenings.

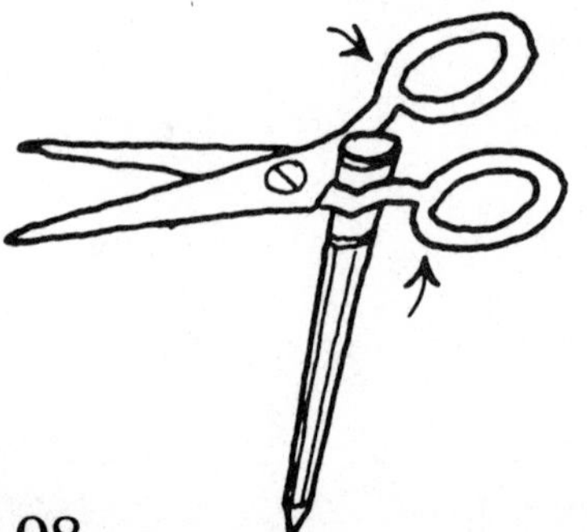

Pencil Eraser Worn Down?

Use the handles of a pair of scissors to squeeze the metal collar of the pencil. The rubber will poke out a little and erase several more times.

Pencils And Erasers

Smudge?
If an eraser smudges your paper, rub it lightly on an extra piece of paper till it's clean.

Pills

What a Pill!
If you have trouble swallowing a pill, take it in a spoonful of jelly or applesauce. Not bad!

Pizza

Pampered Pizza
Take-out pizza is no treat if it's stone-cold by the time you get it home. On a cold night bring along some old newspapers to wrap around the pizza box for the ride home.

Pizza Crackers

This Snack's a Snap.

Rye "Crisp Bread" crackers
Tomato sauce
Cheese

1. Heat oven to 350°F.
2. Put some rye "crisp bread" crackers on a cookie sheet.
3. Spread tomato sauce on each cracker.
4. Put sliced or grated cheese on top.
5. Bake till the cheese is bubbly.

The "crisp bread" softens to be just like real pizza crust.

Pizza

Also . . .
Refrigerator biscuits spread out thin with a rolling pin also make great mini-pizza crusts.

Poison Ivy

Leaves of Three, Let It Be
Poison ivy is a very common wild plant that often causes an itchy rash when touched. Whether you're allergic or not, it's best to stay clear of the three leaved poison ivy vine.

The oil of the poisonous plant is what causes the rash. Touching the oil, then touching another part of your skin, makes the rash spread. If you come in contact with poison ivy, wash with soap and water wherever poison ivy touched. Also, wash anything else that might have touched poison ivy (your clothes, your tools, or your dog, for example).

Relief from Itching
Add one half cup baking soda to your bath water.

Apply a paste made of three parts baking soda and one part water to the rash.

Keep cool. Sweating makes you itch more.

Popcorn

Popcorn for Breakfast?!

Before you butter and salt your next bowl of popcorn, take out a cupful and save it in a plastic bag till morning. At breakfast pour the plain popcorn in a bowl and add some milk and sugar. Puffed corn breakfast cereal!

Posters

Sell!

When you make a poster (“Vote for Me” or “Buy These Cookies” or whatever) remember that your poster should *sell* the idea. Remember the word SELL to remember what a good poster needs:

S . . . . *Simple Shapes.* Clear picture. Recognized from a distance.

E . . . . *Eye Appeal.* Bright colors. Fun to look at.

L . . . . *Letters.* Contrasting to background color. Large. Easy to read from a distance.

L . . . . *Layout.* Words and picture work together. No clutter.

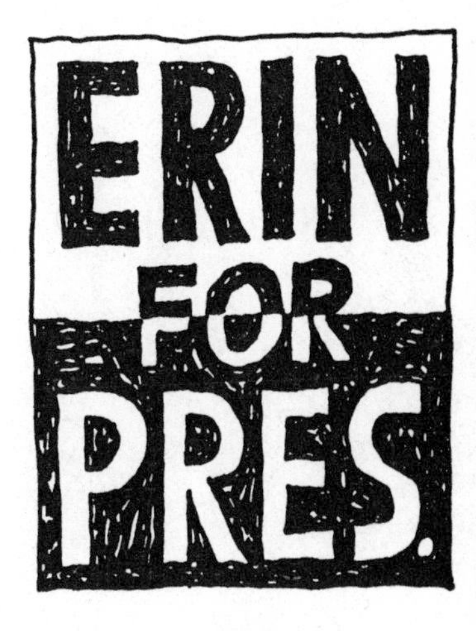

Posters

Win the Next Poster Contest

When designing a poster or booklet cover, make your design on scratch paper first. Cut the various elements apart (title, byline, illustration), then move them around to discover the best looking arrangement. To create the finished design use this first plan as a guide.

Stuck Up

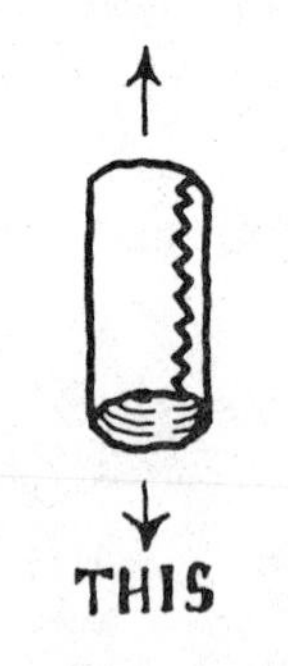

When using masking tape to hang a poster on a wall, the tape need not show. Make little rolls of tape by wrapping it around your finger sticky side out. Stick the tape rolls to the corners of the poster on the back . . . outa sight!

Always attach the tape rolls so that the hollow center points up and down. If the hollow center points left and right, gravity may cause your poster to roll off the wall.

Socks on Your Hands?!

Don't throw away old socks—they can be turned into hand puppets with very little work.

Stage Your Own Shows

You don't need a fancy puppet stage. You can get behind a couch; cover an ironing board or table with a cloth; tack a sheet across a doorway; turn a card table on its side. On with the show!

Can You Stand It?

Store a hand puppet by putting it over an empty bottle. This way your puppet can stand up on your shelf or dresser.

Storing a Marionette

To prevent a marionette's strings from tangling, always store it hanging up. Screw a tiny eye hook into the center of the wooden handle. Hang this from a cup hook attached to the ceiling or a high shelf in a closet.

Quenching Your Thirst

Tried and True

Water quenches thirst better than any other drink. If you're really thirsty, H_2O's the one!

Rainbows

Worth Looking For

When the sun comes out right after a rainfall, a rainbow often appears in the sky. To find it, go outside, turn your back to the sun, and look up in the sky just above the horizon. Look carefully: a real rainbow is softly colored and sometimes only part of it is visible.

Reminding Yourself

You Can't Leave Without It!

If you must remember to take something with you, lean it against or beside the door that you go out. When leaving, you'll be sure to see it and pick it up.

Last Minute Checklist

To avoid that last minute hassle on school mornings, put a checklist on the wall beside the door you go out.

Restrooms

Be In the Know When You're On the Go

When you've got to go, you've got to go! Don't be slowed down by the fact that not all restroom doors are marked "Men" or "Women". Here are some of the signs you might see instead:

BOYS	GIRLS
BRAVES	SQUAWS
BUOYS	GULLS
CABALLEROS	DAMAS
GENTLEMEN	LADIES
GUYS	DOLLS
HIS	HERS
HOMMES	DAMES
JACK	JILL
KINGS	QUEENS
LADS	LASSIES
MONSIEUR	MADEMOISELLE
PAPA	MOMMA
POINTERS	SETTERS
ROMEO	JULIET
SENOR	SENORA
STUDS	FILLIES

Sometimes there is one restroom for both men and women. In this case the door may simply read RESTROOM, or HEAD (on a boat), JOHN, LATRINE (at camp), LAVATORY, TOILET, W.C. or WATER CLOSET.

Running

Wicked Fast

If you ever want to run faster—in a race or just for fun—imagine a great big monster chasing you. Zoooom!

Saving Money

Think Twice

Piggy banks that you have to break in order to get the money out are good to use if you're saving for something special. You'll think twice before you break your piggy bank.

Save First

If you get an allowance, put away a little bit when you first get it. This works much better than saving whatever is left over at the end of the week.

Just Pennies

Decide not to spend any pennies and to save any that you find. Ask for penny rolls at a bank and put the pennies you've collected into the rolls. Pretty soon the pennies will grow into dollars. (If you decide not to spend any dimes, rather than pennies, they'll grow into dollars a lot quicker.)

With Interest

If you can sign your name, you're old enough to open up your own savings account. Ask your mother or father to take you to the bank to start your own account. (*This* is a good time to break your piggy bank. Take the money along.) Then, put a certain amount of money into your account every month. The bank will pay you a small amount of "interest" each month for keeping your money in their bank.

Scary Movies

Eek!

If you get the jitters sitting in a darkened movie theater watching the Creature from the Black Lagoon (and his kind), you'll feel safer if you sit in the back row—nobody can sneak up on you from behind.

Sharks

Sound Advice

Divers who are used to being in the water with sharks around say that the key to safety is staying calm and quiet. If you ever see a shark while swimming in the ocean, try not to splash or scream or attract attention to yourself. Instead, move slowly but steadily to shore . . . THEN scream!!!

Shell Collecting

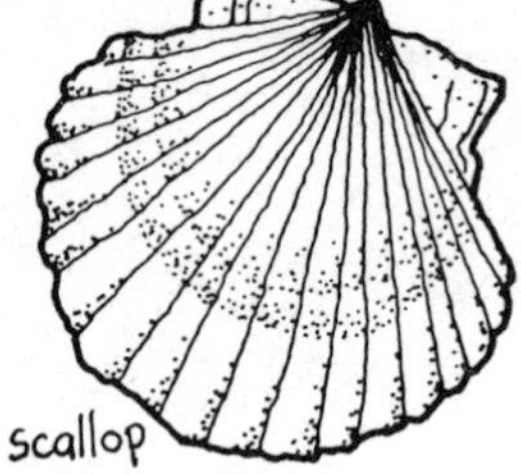

Low Tide for Shell Collecting

The best time for shell collecting is low tide because then less beach is covered by the sea. Times of high and low tides are listed in most local newspapers.

Low tide after a big storm is especially good because more shells than usual are washed up by the storm's big waves.

Colorful When Wet

Many seashells are quite colorful when they're wet but fade as they dry. To keep the shells in your collection looking like they just came out of the sea, coat them with a little baby oil. (This works for beach stones too.)

Shoelaces

Fit To Be Tied

To keep shoelaces tied, wet them a little before you tie them.

Or, tie a double knot: after you make a regular bow knot, tie the two loops together in a simple knot.

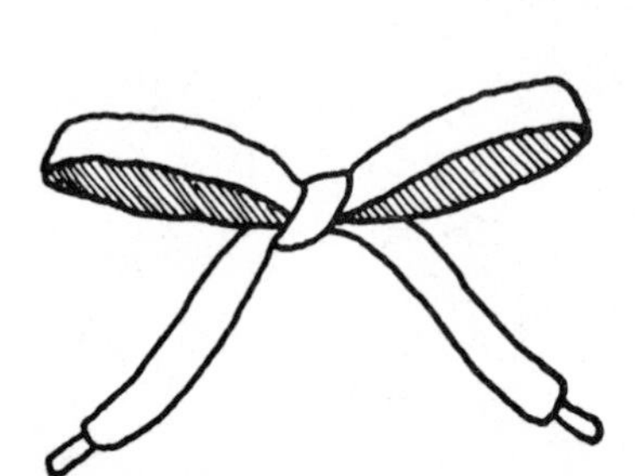

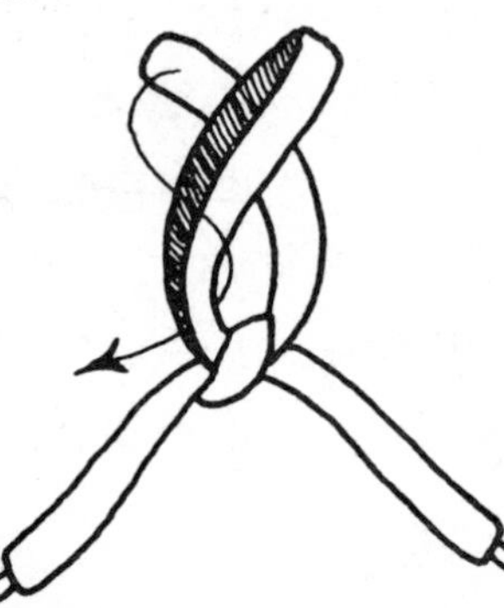

Shoelaces

A Good Tip
If the plastic tip comes off the end of your shoelaces, make a new tip by wrapping a small piece of clear tape around the end.

Not for Sneakers Only
Tie pony tails and braids with fancy new shoelaces.

Shoes

No-Slip Soles
Brand new shoes sometimes have slippery bottoms: scuff up the soles by rubbing them with coarse sandpaper or by shuffling in them on a rough sidewalk.

Shine On!
After applying shoe polish, put old socks on your hands and buff away. Your hands will stay clean, your shoes will get shiny, and you'll have fun too.

If you run out of shoe polish, use petroleum jelly.

Shots

Over In a Jiffy
Hypodermic needles look worse than they feel. When getting a shot, look the other way and count to ten.

Skating

Balancing Act

When first learning to ice skate, carry a hockey stick or a broom to help keep your balance. (In Holland, children start ice skating pushing a chair.)

Toasty Toes

Before putting on your ice skates, breathe into the shoes a few times and they will be warmer.

Tight . . .

To keep skates (or sports shoes) laced tight, put the laces through the holes from the outside to the inside.

But Not Too Tight

When you first put on your skates (or sport shoes) don't lace them too tight or your feet may swell and start hurting. After wearing them awhile pull the laces tighter, but keep them comfortable.

Sky Watching

No Crick In the Neck

The most relaxing position for skywatching, from backyard or terrace, is flat on your back in a sleeping bag. Bring out a pillow (and mosquito repellent!) and stargaze to your heart's content.

City Starscope

You may have trouble seeing stars from the city because of all the bright light at ground level. Cut out the top and bottom of an empty oatmeal or cereal box to use as a starscope. Hold it with hands cupped around your eyes so that all extra light is blocked, and look through it at the stars. See?

Worth Borrowing

If you don't have a telescope, a pair of binoculars is the next best thing for magnifying the moon and stars.

Moon-Eyed

Dates of each month's new moon and full moon are listed in many calendars and most almanacs and daily newspapers.

Left Means Less.

Right? More Tomorrow Night.

If the curve of the crescent shaped moon fits the curve of your left hand, the moon is *waning*—moving away from being *full*.

On the other hand (hee-hee) if the crescent moon fits your right hand the moon is *waxing*—on the way to being *full*.

LEFT means you'll see LESS moon tomorrow.

RIGHT means you'll see MORE moon tomorrow night.

Sleep

Trouble Falling Asleep?
Read awhile before turning out your light to go to sleep.

Relax the parts of your body starting with your toes and moving up: feet, ankles, calves, knees, and so on. Wiggle the parts gently to let the muscles relax. You might get to sleep before you reach your head.

Turn your pillow over to the "cold side".

If all else fails, drink warmed-up milk—a very old cure for insomnia.

Slides

For a Fast Ride on Your Slide
Polish your slide with a sheet of wax paper to make it more slippery.

Or sit on a piece of wax paper and slide down . . . whoosh!

Sneezes

Ah, Ah . . .
If you ever feel the urge to sneeze when you don't want to, whether playing hide-and-seek or making your debut as a star in the school play, here are two ways to keep from sneezing.

Hold a finger right under your nose and press hard against your upper lip.

Or, bite your lip. (*Ouch,* but no *ah-choo.*)

Slipping and Sledding

A large piece of corrugated cardboard makes a good sled for snowy hills (or grassy hills in springtime). Rub soap, paste wax, or parrafin on the bottom for better sledding and for keeping the cardboard dry.

For a Whole Day of Snow Play

Stay outdoors longer by keeping the snow out of your mittens and boots. Ask your mom (or some-one) to wrap extra wide masking tape around the places where your mittens meet your jacket and your pants meet your boots.

Let Your Socks Wear Socks

If your boots aren't waterproof, after you put on your socks slip your feet into plastic bags and then into your boots.

Michelangelo Mittens

Plastic bags over your mittens (held on with not-too-tight elastics) not only keep your hands warm and dry, but are super for smoothing out the sur-face of your next snow sculpture.

Snow

To Build Snow Forts and Sculptures

Start by rolling big balls of snow (as if to make a snowman). Make them as dense as possible. Stack them. If they're too heavy to lift, find something to use as a ramp and slide the balls upward. Pack more snow between them, then smooth out the surface with an ice scraper or snow shovel.

Pack snow in shallow corrugated cardboard boxes. Wet it down with a little water so it packs even tighter, then let it freeze. Turn each box upside-down to remove sturdy snow blocks for building.

Use a snow shovel to cut building blocks of snow from packed down snow drifts.

Invisible Shield

To make your snow fort or sculpture last longer after you have finished building it, cover it with an "ice shield". With a plastic spray bottle, spray water all over its surface.

Snowmazes

Make great walk-through mazes in the snow by stamping trails in your heaviest boots. For dead ends, just reverse direction and retrace your own steps.

You can also make mazes with a snow shovel. If you have the job of shoveling your driveway, this will make it more fun: shovel a maze, play awhile, then shovel off the remaining snow.

Soap Bubble Mix

Make your own soap bubble mix.

Dishwashing liquid
Water

1. In a small dish put one teaspoon of dishwashing liquid.
2. Pour in one quarter cup of water.
3. Stir well with a spoon.

Three Bubble Blowers
Make your own bubble loop with two twist ties (the kind that come with plastic bags).

Dip one end of an empty thread spool in the soap bubble mix and blow gently into the other end.

Cut out the bottom of a small paper cup. Dip one end in the bubble mix and blow through the other. Big bubbles!

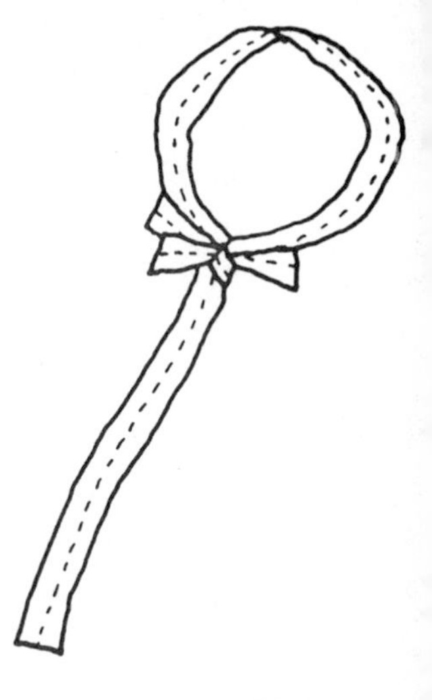

Cool It!
To quickly cool a bowl of too-hot soup, add an ice cube.

Extra, Extra!
Add crunch to your soup by floating popcorn, chips, or broken crackers on top. Why not a whole slice of buttered toast?

Spelling

Spelling Crossword

If you have a Scrabble® game you can use it to learn your list of spelling words and have fun at the same time. Pick out the needed letters and arrange all the words in your spelling list so they criss-cross each other. (If you can't manage *all* the words, do as many as you can.) Now, copy it on paper: a crossword puzzle! When it comes time for the spelling test you'll remember every word!

Some Tips for Hard to Spell Words

If homonyms (words that sound alike, but are spelled differently) are confusing for you, make up a trick to help you remember the spelling of one of them. For example:

- ☐Capitol/Capital
  The U.S. Capit*o*l is a building with a dome. (picture the "o" as a dome.)
- ☐Dessert/Desert
  De*ss*ert has double scoops of ice cream (2 s's).
- ☐Hear/Here
  You h*ear* with your *ear*.
- ☐*Piece/Peace*
  *A pie*ce of *pie* is dessert.
- ☐Principal/Principle
  The school princi*pal* is your *pal*.
- ☐Stationery/Stationary
  Station*er*y is writing pap*er*

Some Hints for Hard to Spell Words

If you have trouble spelling a particular word, try making up a silly phrase to help you remember the right spelling. For example:

☐ Cemetery
Three e's line up like tombstones in a c*e*m*e*t*e*ry.

☐ Secretary
A secret*a*ry can keep *a secret.*

☐ Separate
There's "a rat" in the middle of sep*arat*e.

☐ Surprise
Surprise! No z!

Or make up a silly sentence. For example:

☐ Arithmetic
A *R*at *I*n *Th*e *H*ouse *M*ay *E*at *T*he *I*ce *C*ream.

☐ Geography
*G*eorge *E*dwards' *O*ld *G*randmother *R*ode *A* *P*ig *H*ome *Y*esterday.

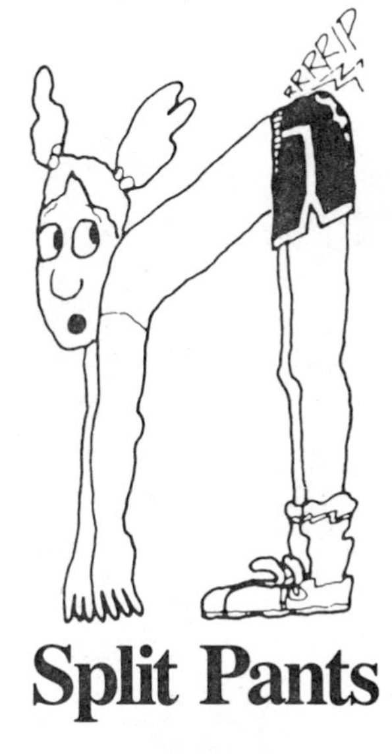

Split Pants

"I See London, I See France . . ."
If you ever split the seat of your pants while you're at school, hide the rip by tying the sleeves of a sweater or jacket around your waist.

Studying

Flash!

Make flash cards to help you study for tests or memorize information. Write a question on the front of an index card, and the answer on back. As you go through the stack, put cards you miss the answer to in a second pile so you can go through them again.

Save for the Future

Keep all your homework papers and quizzes (especially the ones you've flunked) instead of throwing them away. Keep papers for each subject together in a folder. When exam time comes around read through them all as part of your studying. Teachers often ask quiz questions again on exams.

Test Yourself on Tape

If no one is around to help you study for a test, record yourself asking sample test questions on a cassette recorder. Play the questions back, stopping the recorder after each one, and say the answers out loud.

Stuffed Animals

Bath Day for Bears

On a sunny day, give your teddy bear a suds bath:

1. Put some dishwashing detergent in a pan and run some water into it until there's lots of suds.
2. Scoop the suds with your hand and cover your bear with them.
3. Give him a rubdown with a clean, damp wash cloth.
4. Let him stretch out on a towel in the sun to dry. Then brush him to fluff up his fur.

Dry Clean

To clean your bear without using any water, rub him with some cornstarch, then give him a good brushing.

Summer Drinks

Frosted Glasses

Root beer will be extra cold and fantastically foamy if you serve it in frosted glasses. Just leave glasses or glass mugs in the freezer for several hours before pouring in the root beer.

Quick Trick

When your box of chocolate milk mix is almost empty and the little bit of powder left is hard to spoon out, pour a little milk into the box. Swish it around gently and pour into your glass.

Summer Drinks

Fizzy Juice

More fun than just juice.

Ice
Club soda or seltzer water
Fruit juice

1. Put some ice in a glass.
2. Fill half full with club soda or seltzer water.
3. Fill it the rest of the way with any fruit juice—grape, orange, and pineapple are especially tasty.

Teeth

Pearly White

For special occasions when you want your teeth extra white, polish them with a little baking soda and a damp washcloth.

First You Wiggle, Then You Twist

No, it's not a dance! It's the best way to take out a loose tooth. First, wiggle it with your tongue till it's good and loose. Then, with two fingers, turn the tooth around in the same direction until you've twisted it out.

Teeth

Emergency Measures

A knocked-out permanent tooth can often be saved if you act quickly. Put the tooth right back in place if you can. If not, put it in a cup of milk or even water. Then, for the best chance of saving the tooth, get to a dentist within thirty minutes.

Thank You Notes

Short and Sweet

It's easy to write a thank you note if you write it on a picture postcard. There's only enough room for a sentence or two, so all you have to say is "Thank you. I like the gift . . . ", and the colorful picture on the front of the card makes it extra nice to receive.

Double Duty

If a gift comes in the mail, your thank you note serves two purposes: it lets the sender know the package arrived *and* that you liked it.

Try to write thank you notes as soon as possible after receiving a gift—if you put it off, the note may never get written.

Thank You Notes

Worth a Thousand Words

If you'd rather not write a letter, why not draw a picture of you using your new gift? Add a short message (like "Thanks a lot!") and send it in an envelope.

Tipping

Tip!

After a snack or meal at a restaurant you should leave your waiter or waitress a tip. How much? Leave at least fifteen cents for every dollar of the cost of your meal. (If the meal costs three dollars leave three times fifteen cents or forty-five cents.)

TIP	15¢	30¢	45¢	60¢	75¢
COST OF MEAL	$1.00	$2.00	$3.00	$4.00	$5.00

Toasting Marshmallows

Campfire Know-how

Instead of picking up a dead stick from the ground, break a long, young twig from a tree for a marshmallow stick. "Green" twigs won't burn as quickly because they still have water inside.

Flatten the end of the stick on two sides with a jackknife to keep marshmallows from slipping around as you turn the stick.

Place a toasted marshmallow and a bit of chocolate bar in between two graham crackers for a scrumptious dessert sandwich called a "S'more." (Want s'more?)

Tracing

Light Table

If you want to trace a picture onto another piece of paper, hold the blank paper over the picture against a window pane. The daylight shining through the glass should make the picture show up well enough to trace.

Or if you have a glass top table, put a lamp on the floor beneath to make a "light table" for tracing.

Tracing

Write On, Straight Ahead
To keep your writing straight on unlined stationery, put a piece of lined paper underneath. Use a ruler and pen to darken the lines if they don't show through.

All Round
Glasses, saucers, plates, pots and bowls are great for tracing when you need to draw a perfectly round circle but don't have a compass.

Travel Pastimes

Going On a Car Trip?
Plan ahead and take along a few of these things to help pass the time:

- ☐ Binoculars (Look for hawks.)
- ☐ Paper, pencil, and clipboard (Draw. Make up mazes.)
- ☐ Cassette tape player (And earphones)
- ☐ Comics, puzzles, and other books (Read.)
- ☐ Water-filled canteen (Quench your thirst.)
- ☐ Jump rope (Exercise and have fun at rest stops.)
- ☐ Pillow (Sleep.)

On the Look Out

When you're traveling with another kid or anyone who'll play, "look out" games are lots of fun. The idea is to think of an object, then look for it out the car window. The first one who spots it gets the point. Ten points (or however many you wish) wins the game. What sort of things to look for? Anything from out-of-state license plates to Volkswagen "bugs" to wood paneled station wagons to blue bumper stickers to billboards showing people in their bathing suits. You name it!

A - B - See

Look for any object with a name beginning with A ("apple" tree or "airplane"), then go on to B ("barn" or "basketball" hoop), then C, and so on through the alphabet. (Q, X, and Z are toughies—agree ahead to find those letters on signs or billboards.)

Sdrawkcab Sngis Daer

Once you're bored with everything else, try reading signs backwards.

Wet Sneakers

Dry Wet Sneakers

Soaking Wet: Stuff them with crumpled newspaper. Pull out the wet paper and replace it with dry whenever you think of it.

Wet: Fold two wire coat hangers in half and hang your sneakers on them in a dry place.

Damp: Put them in front of the motor vent at the bottom of the refrigerator.

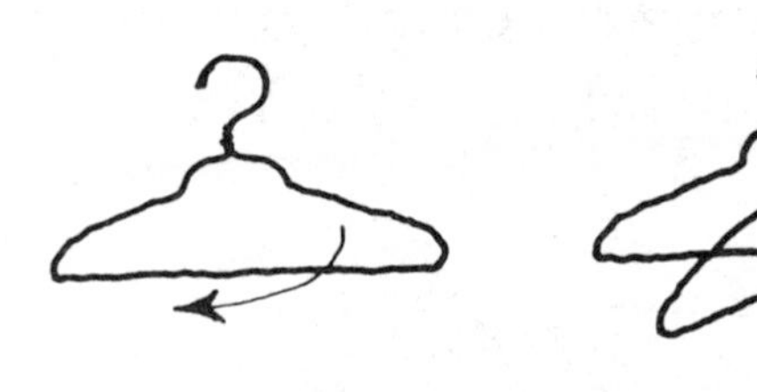

Winter Drinks

Hot Lemonade

A delicious drink for a cold winter's night is hot lemonade, and it's super for soothing a sore throat too. Simply pour boiling water into a tea cup and add lemon juice and honey to suit your taste.

Hot Cider

Apple cider or cranberry juice (or a combination) is delicious heated up.

Especially in December

Make a hot drink extra special by adding a peppermint candy cane or a long cinnamon stick as a stirrer.

Hot Vanilla

Everybody knows what a great warmer-upper hot chocolate is. But did you know you could make hot vanilla?

Milk
Sugar
Vanilla

1. In a saucepan heat up one cup of milk (don't let it boil).
2. Stir in one or two teaspoons of sugar and one-fourth teaspoon vanilla extract.

Zip!
To make a zipper slide easily rub the teeth with a lead pencil or a bar of soap.

XYZ
If you notice your friend's pants are unzipped, quietly say, "XYZ" (Examine Your Zipper).

Give us a hint.

Your hints (and your name) could appear in our next book of "Hints for Kids" or in the "Hints for Kids" newsletter.

Send your hints to:

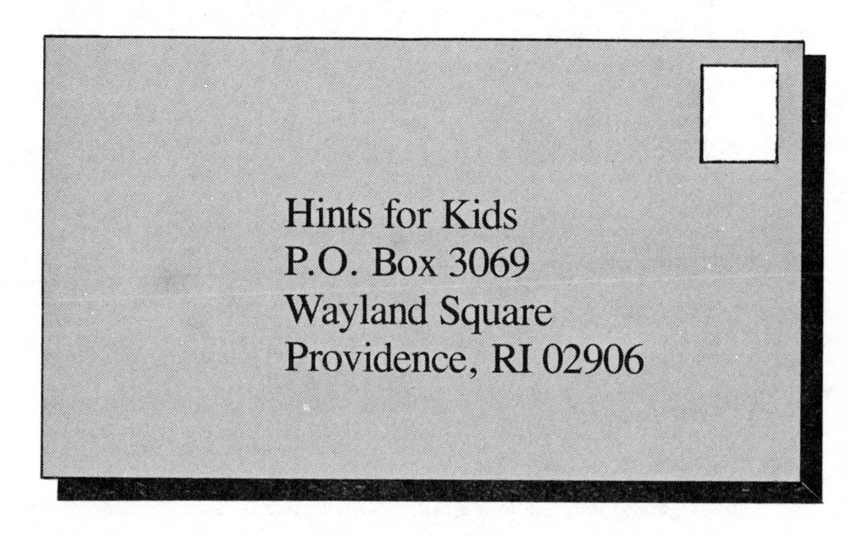

Remember to include a self-addressed stamped envelope, and we'll send you a free copy of the "Hints for Kids" newsletter.